Your Art Is Your Empire

"A Guide For Artists Who Want To Turn Their Dreams Into A Business"

By

Lamont Carey

Editors

Melanee Woodard

Libra Mayo

Rashidah Denton

Cover design

Kia Kellibrew

Published by

LaCarey Entertainment

The Empire Series. Volume 1

ISBN: 978-0-9816200-1-5

Your Art Is Your Empire-A Guide For Artists Who Want To Turn Their Dreams Into A Business.

Vol. 1. The Empire Series

The information provided in this book is designed to provide helpful information on the subjects discussed. The author and publisher are not offering it as legal, accounting, or other professional services advice. In the case of a need for any such expertise consult with the appropriate professional. While best efforts have been used in preparing this book to be as accurate as possible, this book does not contain all information available on the subject. There may be typographical, dated information, or content errors. Therefore, this book should serve only as a general guide and not as the ultimate source of subject information. This book has not been created to be specific to any individual or organizations' situation or needs. The book is intended only to provide information and motivation. References are provided for informational purposes only and do not constitute endorsement of any websites or other sources. Readers should be aware that the websites listed in this book might have changed. The author and publisher shall have no liability or responsibility to any person or entity regarding any loss or damage incurred, or alleged to have incurred, directly or indirectly, by the information contained in this book. You hereby agree to be bound by this disclaimer.

www.lacareyenterprises.com

www.lamontcarey.com

Twitter: @lamontcarey

Distributed Worldwide

Acknowledgements

Pharaoh, Melanee Woodard, Lady Flava, Christine Graham, Iris McLaurin-Southall, Hermond Palmer, Jr., Felicia Bass, Lady Di, Brenda Richardson, Tyrone Hicks, Rashidah Denton, Kevin Hicks, Valerie White, Afi, Charles Mitchell, Dyone Mitchell, Joe Gorham, Monday Childs, Kimberly Washington, and my social network family, my fans, and any and everyone I forgot.

Dear Reader,

I wrote this book with the hopes that you can learn from my mistakes and benefit from my successes. I've learned to evaluate my experiences to better understand myself and to empower others. Being an artist sometimes feels like we are the most underappreciated and undervalued, but art exist everywhere and in every walk of life! We create a greater understanding of a complex existence but so many of us die broke.

Art is a business whether you profit from it or someone else who is business savvy does. We have to learn to value our work, market our work and make money from our work. The only way for us to capitalize off of our work is to educate ourselves about the business of art.

I am not a lawyer or a business guru so this isn't legal advice. I am just a full time artist that has been finding ways to position myself to continually profit from my creations. I have had a tremendous amount of success in making my work visible, obtainable and profitable. However, I have made an enormous amount of mistakes because I wasn't treating my art as a business and I didn't know how to operate as a businessman who happens to be an artist. I started out as an artist hoping someone would discover me and pay me. Until I changed my thinking about business, I was not progressing.

This book is designed to show you how I turned my way of thinking and acting about my artistic expressions. Some of my experiences you may recognize, some you will not and some you may be able to apply to your journey. I just want you to be successful. I hope this book has a positive impact on you and your journey to positioning yourself as a businessperson whose business is art.

Remember Your Art Is Your Empire. **You must protect it.**

Table of Contents

Art is engrained in our lives from textbooks to license plates. Let's use the eBook as an example. Someone wrote the text, someone designed the covers and someone illustrated or photographed the images inside the book. The bigger challenge was protecting the work, marketing the work to schools, and securing distribution of the books. This is what we will be exploring in this book that I wrote; Kia designed the cover, Rashidah took the picture, Melanee, Libra and Rashidah edited the manuscript and Melanee and I, through my company, LaCarey Enterprises, were able to market and distribute it so that you are able to read it now!

Chapter 1

Becoming a Full Time Artist

I will assume that you are considering becoming a full-time artist. These will probably be the most complex questions that you will have to answer because they will be life changing. To be honest, you should base this decision on several factors that include, but are not limited to, the following:

Do you have a product or service?

Do you believe you can make money from your products or services?

Do you really just want people to hear what's on your heart or do you want to get paid for your art?

Are you comfortable asking people to pay you for your work?

What are your goals?

Is one of your goals to become wealthy?

Are you currently making enough money from art to live off of?

How much money do you have saved to sustain your lifestyle until you begin earning an income?

Have your family members or friends agreed to support you financially while you pursue your dreams?

Do you have some kind of contractual agreement or advance from a company that will kick in to sustain your current lifestyle?

Are you self-motivating?

Is your art currently protected?

Those are some questions you should seriously be asking yourself. You will have to find answers for the majority of the questions beforehand but certainly during your life as a full-time artist.

This book will touch on many of those questions. I was unfortunately forced to discover all of this after desperately trying to figure out how to maintain my basic needs of food and shelter. In addition, I learned that there were other steps I needed to secure before I could make the kind of money I needed to stay a full-time artist. So, there is a bright side to all of this and together we're going to prepare you for success.

Now we know entertainment is a global multi-billion dollar industry. People have enjoyed the arts for centuries and artists across the world have been successful at making a living from their craft. Opportunities are unlimited and we need to be prepared for those that appear and take advantage of the ones that exist.

First, let's see if you are mentally prepared to take on the world. Right now you may be full of excitement. You can't wait to tell the world that being an artist is your full-time gig. Sooner than later, you will get frustrated because the world is not praising you the way you feel you should be praised. You'll find yourself second-guessing the audience's intelligence. You'll compare your work to other artists who seem to be getting most of the attention. You'll then question your work. You may experience some jealousy on your part. You'll question your approach. You may even begin to mimic their style of art. Plus, your family and friends will be whispering in your ear or behind your back telling you that you're wasting your time. In other words, you're not that good. If you let those feelings and opinions sink in, you will either begin to believe all the voices inside and outside of your head and will quit or, that determination to silence them and succeed will kick in. If determination kicks in, you will keep doing it your way. That's what makes your work unique.

You'll pat yourself on your own back and chant, "They can't stop me!" Finally, you will declare to blow minds every time you take the stage or show your work. Subconsciously or consciously, you will formulate a plan to succeed. Your energy and determination is on fire. BAM! You're ready to take on the world.

Hold up. Energy is lovely. However, this is a business. Mesmerizing every audience is golden and it will get you further. Again this is a business. So your plan of action should include how to do the business of art.

So, let's slow down and decide if you are going to become a full-time artist. Everything mentioned so far fits into the equation as you decide your future. Literarily, your art is your empire or your poor house. The more frequently you can secure paying gigs the more fulfilled you may feel. You must create, protect, and profit from it. That's what business owners do. If you're not able to line up paying gigs then maybe today isn't the day to quit your job to become a full-time artist. Now if you have some money in your savings or have the financial support from your loved ones, I say go for it. I know. I know. You are very talented. Your talent isn't even a factor that I have considered. I believe your talent is exceptional and your ability to be successful is undeniable. I just know every month rent/mortgage and your phone bill has to be paid.

Plus, you have to eat every day. I just don't want to see you at a traffic intersection shaking a dirty change cup at my car window. I would really hate to look away like I don't even see you.

This doesn't mean you can't be a professional artist right now. I just need you to be focused on making an income. I know many artists who are not interested in making money or it is not the driving force for being an artist. They want to share their life experiences to help others find their way to happiness or solve problems. That's so beautiful and I commend those of you who want to help and heal the world. My focus is on helping you prepare to make money. Did you know that you could still help and heal the world and make an income? This book can help you do that or you can use it as a guide in your efforts to gain more exposure. My focus is on helping you turn Your Art Into An Empire because a full-time artist needs to get paid. The best way I know how to do that is to tell you all that I have gone through…and I am ready to do just that. Right now!

Now that you've confirmed your decision of becoming an artist full-time, let's take a step back and take a look at the things that should be considered and confronted. In this unlimited world of opportunities, you have to factor in your competition. You are not only competing against the artists you see in your area but you are competing globally with every performing artist that exists. People who are considering hiring you to showcase may be considering your craft, your following, and your prices, but they want to get the best artist their money can buy. This is not to discourage you…just the truth. I overcame those obstacles. I did this by not focusing on my competition but on my craft, learning from my mistakes, and positioning myself in the right places at the right times. You will reap the benefits from those lessons.

Most new artists are told or feel they have to pay dues. I personally don't understand that train of thought but I bought into it. The translation is that you are expected to do free appearances until you or your peers feel you should get paid for your talent. Some of your peers would rather see you at that stop light shaking that change cup at me.

I say, "The hell with that! Pay me! You want me to perform at your event and YOU are charging! Pay me!" If I had known then what I know now, I would have approached every situation as a businessman. Start getting paid as soon as the opportunities arise! Your talents are always worthy of payment. Now there are some cases where you may want to consider if it is worth doing a gig for free. My thinking is that there are no "free" gigs. It has to be a benefit to you in furthering your efforts in accomplishing your goals; for example, you are offered an opportunity to perform at a national board of education conference. There will be 500 school representatives from schools across the country. I suggest you take this opportunity if your goal is to start getting paid to provide services to students such as books, workshops, motivational speeches, and performances. This one opportunity can provide you access to every school in your country. Even if you don't get in all of them and only get in 10% of the schools, that's 50 schools!

I would also suggest that you speak or perform in front of that audience of representatives. The chances of obtaining paying gigs are great because oftentimes these are the persons that make the financial decisions or who can influence the decision makers. Presenting in a room where you don't know who is in the audience can be challenging, if you are not able to determine the professional positions they may hold. I'm not saying you can't secure a gig in this kind of audience but the chances are not as great. So, you have to decide what's in your best interest. No one else can do that for you. However, I will assist you with identifying potential situations that may be opportunities as we progress through this book.

As I mentioned before, you should weigh the decision on becoming a full-time artist on your ability to eat food every day, keep a roof over your head, your available resources, your opportunities, your current financial commitments, threats that exist in your life and business, and the reality of where you are in your career. Don't feel like you are less of an artist because you have to keep your full-time job. This doesn't make your art a hobby. It actually makes you a smart businessperson. You are being realistic. I didn't weigh those options. I felt my talents would support me. A few months after, I realized, ramen noodles didn't taste anything like those steaks I was used to eating. A little while after that I was back at Mom's house with my jaws sunk in and my pride damaged. Now if you know me, you know my ribs and heartbeat are visible through my t-shirt, so I was too small to be losing weight! However, I was determined to make it just like you are now. So whatever you decide, we are going to make it happen. You can get a case of noodles for like $5. You get 24 in the case. Now you will have to go back to drinking faucet water for a while because the next time you'll be drinking spring water will be when you end up next to a stream. In that case, you should keep that change cup handy! Yes, sacrifices are a must. Life of a struggling artist isn't a joke. You will be taking "a vow of poverty" until you make the money come in. You can do it!

Something else you should take into consideration before you make your decision is the truth about yourself. There are no limitations in your genre. However, you can be your biggest obstacle. No perceived or visible handicaps work here. You just have to be mentally ready to take on the task of being the director of your path. Your success or failure depends completely on you. What you put into your career is what you will get out of it. So how motivated are you to do what it takes to succeed? You have to be honest with yourself. If you are lazy, this could be a major issue. However, your passion should kick you into overdrive. It has to because being a full time artist demands more of your time than a 9-5 where you are working for someone else. If you aren't selling as an artist, you aren't eating. Even though you're one individual, you are still a business. To be a successful artist you have to spend countless time making phone calls to try and secure opportunities. You have to constantly market yourself online, offline, attending events, securing interviews, creating artistic pieces, performing, and networking your behind off. As a full-time artist, you are the Chief Executive Officer (CEO), Chief Financial Officer (CFO), Marketing Department and the Administrative Assistant. You have to wear all of these hats until you can build you a team to help out. You will build that team!

Are you still motivated? Well, pump your fist in the air and let's get down to business!

Chapter 2

Planning For Success

Now…you need a plan. This is a big step that will change the rest of your life. I didn't have a plan and I made a lot of mistakes. You will benefit from those lessons because you will have a plan; you will be a triple threat. See, you have my mistakes to look at so you know what to avoid, you have your plan, and you have your talents. Whew! You're going to shut them down!

Look, don't be intimidated by the idea of creating a plan. I was terrified of doing it. It was easy for me to dismiss it and say, "I don't need a plan; my talent is all I need." The truth is that I didn't know anything about writing a plan. I didn't understand why I would need one. Plus, I figured it would take too much time to create one and I wanted to start making money now. So I counseled myself on a business that I knew nothing about. This was my rationalization and conversation with me "Audiences already love my two poems! All I have to do is spit/ perform and the whole world will fall in love with me." And this thought came after only two people asked me did I have a CD for sale! A couple days later, I ran into a studio and free-styled my whole CD in one day with no music. I figured this would be raw spoken word. To be honest, I didn't know anything about buying tracks or creating a CD. I didn't even know how long a poem should be. I didn't even know how to write a poem. I was in the studio telling the engineer to name a topic or give me a word. This is how I created my first CD entitled IMAGINE. All I knew to do was stand in front of a microphone and spit/recite. This attitude set me back years. This naïveté allowed me to get pimped by promoters. This cockiness allowed me to put out a book that was edited by someone who failed English too! This ego allowed poetry pimps to get me to purchase a lot of merchandise I didn't need or if I needed it, I didn't know how to use it. This fear allowed me to rush everything. The reason I was rushing was because I never looked at it as running a business. I never even considered that I was a full-time artist. I was chasing the stage. I was chasing the applause. I was rushing because I was loving what I was doing and people seemed to love it too. So I jumped in with nothing but two poems, an ego, and a little money in my pocket. In my defense, that same CD has provided me every opportunity that I have today. Some would say I was lucky, but I worked hard for every opportunity that I secured. The point being, if I had a plan, I would have been more focused on the right steps versus any steps. As long as I was performing, I thought I was doing what I needed to do. Another thing that was damaging was that saying, "You have to spend money to make money." The truth is you have to spend money but on the right stuff that is going to make you money. If you don't know what you are supposed to spend money on, anyone can tell you what to spend it on. I lived it and they loved me for it! People say "A sucker is born everyday" and I was born a rainbow-colored lollipop with bubblegum in the center. I was getting chewed out! With that said, I am going to give you some great steps and things you need to do in this BUSINESS.

You NEED a plan. I don't mean you need a three hundred-page business plan, at this point. However, you should have at least an outline with a description of all the things you feel you need to do to be successful at booking gigs. This outline should include (1) your overall vision/what you want to accomplish as an artist, (2) the short-term goals that will bring you closer to accomplishing that long-term goal. You can start off by creating a weekly, monthly, or yearly plan. You can write it in a journal, type it or however you want to jot it down. I will suggest that you put your weekly goals on a calendar on the wall or on your phone. Now if you create your plan on electronic devices, please save them on a thumb drive. I can't tell you how many times computers crashed or cell phones got lost, dropped in the toilet, baby slobbering on it or simply stolen. Always create a backup copy.

With an outline or plan, you can check off what you have accomplished. By checking off each goal, you can monitor your progress. Seeing these accomplishments will boost your confidence. Seeing and feeling that is MO-TI-VATION! You can also revise your plan as often as you like to meet the changes of your journey. You may accomplish some things faster than you predicted, delete steps that you later feel don't fit into your plan, or you can

20

add new goals and objectives. This is your plan. You do it to keep yourself focused and on track. I will say, "be honest with you." If you feel the need to create another document for others to find so they think your ambition is bigger, do that! Fake it until you make it but don't trick yourself. Do I hear that change cup SHAKING?

Now let's protect art!

Chapter 3

The Beauty of Copyrighting

I thought being a spoken word artist was the easiest career move and easiest business to start because I didn't need any money down! All I had to do was find opportunities to recites or spit! Majority of the time I didn't even need a microphone. All I required was an audience. Well, I don't think like that anymore. Money is needed. Not a lot of capital is needed, but money is definitely needed. If you don't have to spend money on anything else, you should spend it on getting your work; {intellectual property} COPYRIGHTED! Now the copyright office says, your work is protected the minute it is created and fixed in a tangible form. We're not going to depend on that! Register your stuff with the copyright office. This way you will have proof of the date it was created, just in case someone steals your work, and tries to claim it, as theirs. [1]The additional benefit is that your work will be protected throughout your lifetime plus 75 years after your death! This type of protection is worth it and it will cost you a little more if you mail it in compared to doing it online. So it is cheaper to upload electronic copies of your work and

---

[1] Check with the Copyright Office to make sure this remains the policy.

you still receive the same protection. Now get this, if you mail it in, your work is protected the moment the post office stamps the envelope! !

I won't assume you know what copyrighting is so I will take a few steps back to explain based on my understanding. Copyright, is a form of law, which is put in place to protect your original works which includes poetry, books, films, plays, movies, movies, etc. The legal term for original work is, intellectual property. It does not protect ideas, systems, and facts, but it does protect the way things are expressed. Note that copyrighting is not the same as having a trademark. Trade marking is different. I am not covering trademarks in this book. You will have to do further research.

Please understand that getting your stuff copyrighted does not stop people from stealing and using your work. If you were to find out that someone was illegally using or selling your work as his or hers, having your intellectual property copyrighted can prove your ownership in litigation. The security is in the date your work was copyrighted. By having your work registered, you can prove your intellectual property existed before the crooks got their hands on it.

Now, it will be extremely complicated or may not even be possible, to prove ownership if your work isn't registered with a credible institution like The Library of Congress-Copyright Office. I know a lot of us like to post new pieces of our work online so our social network peers can give us their input before we decide to include the work in our catalog. That's not a good idea. In social networks, anybody can see your work. Let's say you put your artistry out there for feedback and one of your friends-who you aren't close with or barely even know- decides to add this piece to their new book and get it copyrighted that day. How can you prove it's your work? If you didn't register your piece, it becomes theirs because you can't prove that you are the original owner. If you've registered the work beforehand and they have registered after you did, who is the owner? Yup, you are.

Another example where having your work registered could have helped prove ownership: Let's say you have been performing this certain piece around town and another artist learns every word, records it, and copyrights it, how can you prove that original piece is your creation? Are the memories of the people who heard you perform said piece countless times, reliable enough to accurately testify on the date you created it? Can they recall the date they first heard you recite the work?

Always register your intellectual property before you present it to the public in any format. If you protect your work, it should increase the chances of a judgment by the courts going in the favor of the original owner. The

24

thief would have to stop using your work, pay you damages, and royalty fees! Remember, this is your business and part of your estate. You should be compensated for the use of your work. Your heirs should be compensated for the use of your work after your death. Think about how much money Michael Jackson's family, Elvis Presley's family, and Tupac's family are collecting from royalties. Their work was protected. Their families are still reaping the benefits from a business decision the artist made to copyright their work.

Another thing that you have to look into when you start posting online is international copyrights laws and how to protect your work globally. The information I am providing in this book covers the U.S. and other countries that acknowledge U.S. laws. Most countries supposedly respect these laws but double check. I know you have seen those fake name brand bags, right? Yeah. So you want to make sure your work is protected in that country!

Some folks who don't have enough money to register with the Copyright Office, they do the "Poor man's" copyright. I really do not agree with this as a form of proof of creation of original work. However I am going to mention this because some of you have probably been told to do it this way. Typically how this works is, you put your work in an envelope and mail it to yourself. The problem that I have with this is that there isn't any proof when your work was created that can't be contested.

To add, it is a known fact that people have been accused of holding the envelope over boiling water or putting it in a microwave for a few minutes so heat will allow you to open and reseal mail. Anyway, that is why I don't trust that. When registering with the Copyright office you will have a copy of your work on file and you will receive a Certificate of Registration. We lose things all the time, so you don't want to chance the poor man's copyright as a long-term solution. Plus, as a full time artist you may be evicted a few times before the money starts to flow in. Sike!

Here is another cheap way to copyright your work. Let's say you have tons of your art that you need copyrighted. You can barely afford to get one or maybe even two of them done so getting all of them protected seem impossible. Do not panic. Here is a way to copyright them all together. Remember the table of contents in the last book you read? You can take that approach. You will create a title and a table of contents that lists the title of each piece. Now, when you start publishing them separately, you need to copyright them in the in the new category. For example, if you decided to copyright two hundred poems out of that five hundred, you should copyright that as a new book. There is a section on the form that will ask you if the new work is derived from a previously published or copyrighted material. Your answer would be, "Yes". You will then reference the 200 poems as a derivative from the 500 poems you originally copyrighted.

So in a nutshell, copyright **all** of your intellectual property before you show or allow anyone to hear it. Registering your work with the Library of Congress-Copyright Office will prove you are the owner of this work in a court of law. With this proof of ownership, you can shoot the violator a cease and desist order. If they continue using your work, you can sue. Or you can choose to sue and recoup a percentage of money earned off the sale of your intellectual property, if not all of it. See, a cease and desist order is really a legal document that you use to demand that an entity stops doing or continuing to do a certain activity. It is basically a letter threatening that if they do not stop using your work, you will sue. If you don't do this, all you can do and will do is complain.

I am actually dealing with a copyright issue now. An artist used not only my words, but also my voice on his album. He didn't even give me name credit or a dime for my work. However my work was already copyrighted. So this looks good for the old boy.

Another thing to remain mindful of is that there is nothing new under the sun. Nothing is identical either, not even identical twins. You will encounter other artists whose work has the same concepts or maybe even a line similar to yours. You have to contact the Copyright Office to find out what percentage that has to be different from yours.

Visit the Library of Congress-Copyright Office's website at www.copyright.gov. Read and follow the instructions listed on the site. You can download forms, print them, file online, or have them sent to you. Trust me, this process is more than worth the money. Your favorite stars and up and coming stars protect themselves there. Register and have your work cataloged alongside your favorite superstar.

I don't usually promote any company that can afford to pay me. However, I wanted to make sure you start your journey off protected.

Please don't dismiss this. If you want to make money off your art, you'd want to secure it. Every dollar counts, especially if you are a full-time artist.

Chapter 4

Should You Pay The MAN (Taxes)

Now you might be one of those revolutionary artists, who are not going to pay the MAN (also known as the Government) anything. I bow my head and hold my fist in the air because I understand your pain. I love that you're passionate about what you feel. But, can I ask you a question? Have you ever heard of Redd Foxx, Richard Pryor, Lamont Carey, and Wesley Snipes? Yeah. We thought that too. Yep, they got me! They had me in there trying to decide if I wanted to faint or play dead. The examiner saw me weighing my options and decided to help me. He said, "Mr. Carey, I'm wondering if you are money laundering. You don't have a lot of receipts, no real records, but you say you only made such and such this year? Mr. Carey, you just bought a BMW, correct?" "Long story short, I walked out there owing them money, penalties, and interest. Deep inside, I felt like I was robbed, but I walked out of there wanting to twirl on my tippy toes like a ballerina. I was excited not to be going to jail, even though I didn't break the law!

The point is you have to keep accurate records. Most artists starting out can't afford to hire a bookkeeper/accountant. However, you are still responsible for paying taxes. You should want to learn how to keep records, so you can monitor how much money you have coming in and what you are spending your money on. This will be your way of evaluating if this business venture is profitable. The IRS only cares if you are paying your share of taxes. They demand a cut off of that gig you just got paid to do. I know it seems unfair because you are just starting out and you only got paid a little money. I know. I know your pain. However, these folks will pull up on you at that intersection and take that money right out of your "change cup", take your cup, and your clothes! I know I am very extreme. I am really not trying to scare you. I just want you to avoid this entire situation. We all know the IRS has been known to repossess every tangible possession they believe they can auction off for sale to recoup the money owed to them in taxes. They are also notorious for sending delinquent folks to prison.

My suggestion is that you look into purchasing some bookkeeping software, learn it, and use it. You can even find some reasonably priced bookkeeping classes, to learn how to keep track of your money coming in and going out. Regardless, if you don't do any of those suggestions, **keep ALL your receipts up to 7 years**. If the IRS ever audits you, you can show your income and expenses. When you become a full time artist you will not receive tax papers from your employer. You are the employer! The IRS is your employee. They want to be paid all of their money…on time!

Most artists starting out will be paid in cash. This is also called, "being paid under the table". This really isn't good. Who wants to turn down cash especially when some people's checks bounce? Cash always looks good. However, there is no proof this transaction ever took place. So, in the eyes of the government, this is wrong. I know you will pay taxes on this money. Now if you don't write down that you received this money, you may forget about it. Remember you didn't get a receipt.

I had no intentions on cheating the IRS out of anything. I was proud to be in business. I was looking forward to paying taxes. To this day, I know I didn't make all the money they accused me of making. However, I was paid in cash a lot. I couldn't prove all of my income, because I didn't have all the receipts to reflect my exact income. I know it would have been just as hard for them to prove I made all of the money they said, but I didn't want to be under any investigation, sitting in jail, or going to court.

There are several ways you can avoid this situation. Either you refuse to take cash, or you can go and purchase receipt books from a business supply store. The next time you receive cash, you can write out a receipt that details all of the information pertaining to this event and give it to your client. You should list what company paid you, date, how much, location, and whatever else you deem important information. Also, have them sign it.

When you agree to do the event, you should create an invoice of the agreed amount, the date, time, location, what services they are hiring you for, how long you are required to perform, and when you expect to be paid. You can even suggest the kind of payment that you and your Company prefer to accept. Once you are paid, forward them a thank you letter for their payment. If paid in cash, you can state in the email that they paid you in cash but you wanted them to have a record of the business transaction as well.

Most computers come with software with templates of forms such as invoices already installed. You can customize those invoices to your liking, or simply use the template. Another option is to do an Internet search of sample invoices and mimic what you see but include your information in the suggested locations.

Another problem you want to avoid with taxes is filling out a W-9 form and not paying your taxes. A W-9 form is a tax form that most organizations will have you fill out and sign to cover themselves and show that they paid you a certain amount of money for services rendered. If you don't pay your taxes on that money, the IRS has a copy of that form! That is proof that you made that money.

Lately, one of the things I did was start my company, LaCarey Entertainment, LLC. I later changed the name to LaCarey Enterprises. This enabled me to pay sales taxes every month. We will discuss this process in Chapter 5.

Chapter 5

Getting Down To Business

Another thing you should consider is becoming and registering as a business. I know this may seem out of the scope of your immediate plans. But I know if you are considering being a full time artist, you have imagined owning a business! You probably already thought of the name, logo, and envisioned it at its peak of success!

Let me make you aware of one thing, technically in your state, you could be considered as operating an illegal business if you are engaging in the selling of your talents and products in exchange for money. I want you to be legit. Find out what your state's definition of operating a business. This could subject you to fines, penalties, and interest that you really don't want to be paying! I don't know how they are able to divide one violation into three, but they do! You don't want to be paying anyone any unnecessary money. Your goal is to make money!

So what I did was start a home-based business. This made my life a whole lot simpler in a few ways.

I was already conducting business as an independent artist. This made me legit in the eyes of the government.

By becoming a home-based business, I am able to write-off a percentage of my regular bills as a business expense because I need to use electricity, water, AC/Heat, space, phone, alarm system, and more to run my business. It is required by law that I identify a section of my home that will be used as my work area (the rest is considered living space) as a tax write-off for the business. I save money in the end. The more money I save in taxes, the more money I keep! You see my point?

Starting the business taught me that I could start paying taxes more often than once a year. Businesses can pay quarterly and retail sales taxes can be paid monthly. Paying taxes this way meant I couldn't forget how much I was suppose to pay at the beginning of the next year. I was able to pay it the same month I made it. This was huge for me.

My biggest problem with taxes is that I kept bad records, or no records at all. That's how I ended up in that IRS office with tears in my eyes. You can't pay something you don't remember you owe. The hardest thing for me to do was keep track of receipts even though I tried. I started stuffing them in bags, drawers and laptop cases. When I needed the receipts, I had them. However, every time I looked at that pile of paper, I realized I didn't want to be ruffling through that! I would just carry the containers to the tax person to figure out. I know it's horrible but you see my point? I was unorganized, messy, unprofessional, and losing money. How was I going to be able to determine if I was making more money than I was spending if I didn't even want to add up the receipts? I had no clue as to what the total was that I was spending. I just thought if I can pay all my bills, buy supplies, keep booking gigs, and keep money in my bank account, I was good. I wasn't even thinking about the IRS until they told me I owed them some money that I couldn't prove that I didn't owe. Nothing changes me like being robbed. So being able to pay my taxes sooner was the last element that encouraged me to start the business. Plus considering starting an entertainment company motivated me and I was excited to be adding CEO or President behind my name. I think I slammed my door a few times just to get the feel of this new power. BAM! Get to work or you are out of here on your backside! You'll never work in this town again!

I started researching what kind of business that I wanted to start. A nonprofit wouldn't work because I was trying to get PAID. After the assistance of an amazing businesswoman, we decided that a Limited Liability Corporation (LLC) was the best way for me to go. This status allowed me to operate like a business but be able to file taxes as an individual. The LLC also allowed me to protect my personal assets from my business. For instance, if my company was sued and I lost, they can only take assets associated with my business and not my personal assets. Starting a sole proprietorship wouldn't provide me that same protection of my personal assets if my company were sued. Now the goal is to never getting sued but people sue folks for anything and everything. I also didn't want to start a regular corporation because I could be voted out of my company by the elected board members. Not happening! This is a dictatorship! You will not be handing me a pink slip in the company that I built. BAM! (Slamming the door). You'll never work in this town again!

Another benefit to starting a Limited Liability Corporation was it allowed me to setup a quicker way to pay sales taxes every month with my state. This was awesome for me because I could deduct the percentages that I owe off each gig and put it in my bank account until it was time to pay my sales taxes for the month. This was very convenient for me to pay every month because if not, I could easily spend that money by accident or on purpose. My next gig was never guaranteed, so if I didn't get a gig, I will use the money that I have saved to pay what I need to pay to survive.

I know some folks will say that was a bad idea to pay taxes every month because I could use that money to invest back into my business. Smart idea. However, I knew I was bad at keeping records. So my solution was paying these people while I have the money. After I give them their money, I dump the receipts into my receipt graveyard.

You should keep your receipts for seven (7) years just in case the "MAN/IRS" comes knocking. You can choose to pay your taxes this way until you become better at keeping records or hiring an accountant. For now, it'll keep you out of jail!

Starting LaCarey Entertainment, LLC was a great thing for me. However, it may not be the best thing for you to do. I suggest that you look into what it takes to start a business in your state by contacting the government agency that handles that. You can also consult with a business lawyer on what would be the best business structure for you to start. If you are just starting out as a full time artist, I recommend you contact the government agency that handles business licenses in your state. You may even be able to pull this information up online. You probably can even download the applications, too. To obtain a consultant will cost you. Investigate if there is any organizations in your area that help individuals setup a business for free. There are several in Washington, DC, so I am sure there may be at least one in your area.

It was pretty easy for me to setup my business. I called the IRS at (866) 816-2065 to get my Employers Identification Number (EIN). Next I went to the Consumer and Regulatory Affairs office, registered my business, and paid for my business license. I did it all in one day! I am not sure if it is this simple and easy in your state. You should do more research. I know the District of Columbia charges an additional fee for expediting the process to be done in one day. I believe the fee is to encourage people to do all of this online.

Either way, there were more benefits to me starting a business than there was for me not to. You will basically be a business whether you see yourself as one or not. The problem comes into play if the US Government or your state government sees you as a business but not as a legit one! I know you have read or heard the politicians complaining about how some businesses don't pay their fair share of taxes. Just be mindful. The IRS will come and get you and your cup off that intersection.

The last note for this chapter; make sure you know what business structure you intend to setup before you register to get an EIN. States recognize LLCs but the IRS doesn't recognize you as that unless you have employees. They recognize you as an individual. This is how you are able to file your business taxes along with your personal income. You need to be clear with them when seeking your LLC so your company name is listed instead of your birth name. I did this and I was listed as Lamont Carey doing business as LaCarey Entertainment, LLC therefore the IRS considered me a sole proprietorship. This created problems when a company that was hiring me had me to fill out a W9 form in order for the IRS to be notified that they paid me. The form was being rejected because I would fill it out to LaCarey Entertainment, LLC and the IRS only identified

Lamont Carey. I had to start filling the form out as Lamont Carey with my social security number versus my company name and my EIN. So make sure you are clear that you are registering your company as an LLC. The IRS will have you as a one-member LLC. Remember the benefit of structuring your company, as a LLC is to protect your personal assets from your business assets. Again, be sure your state recognizes your LLC status.

Chapter 6

The Art of Selling

There are several skill sets you will need in order to be a successful full-time artist and I believe selling is 90% of it. Selling is the beginning and the end of every business and social connection. Think about this: we had to sell ourselves to strangers before they became our friends. We had to sell ourselves to our significant others before they gave us their phone numbers. Or think about when you have met someone and you walk away feeling like that person didn't like you. You may have said, "I don't understand how this person doesn't like me. I was polite. I was friendly. I even laughed at those boring jokes." You clearly felt you were presenting your best qualities but this person didn't buy it. You may have been doing it unconsciously but you were trying to make a sell.

Each of the examples could have been the beginning or the end of a long-term business relationship versus just a personal one. People buy stuff from individuals or brands they like and trust. First impressions are extremely important to building relationships and your success as a full time artist. If one person likes you, chances are they will say something favorable about their experience with you to someone they know. That also applies if they don't like you! You need for them to like you. You have to be able to connect to folks. Most of us are good at befriending people. If you are not good at it, you can learn. I am not saying that you have to be phony. Your likability just has to outweigh the folks who don't like you. You are your product and brand when you are a full time artist. So you are always selling. I just need you to start learning how to do it better.

You probably cringed at the thought of having to sell. Most of us have unfavorable images of salespeople. I know my initial images of salesmen are of a dirty addict trying to sell me an old microwave oven with no cord or a shady-looking sharply dressed character with his shirt unbuttoned with a gold chain around his neck that is being swallowed by bushy salt and pepper chest hairs, or the old guy with the suit from 1962 that knocks at my door to sell me encyclopedias. Those folks do exist. However, we encounter salespeople every day and all day. We even go looking for them. Take a look around the area where you are. The majority of everything you own was sold to you by someone, even this book.

Salespeople are not the enemy. We exist to make people happier by assisting them in acquiring the things they want, need, or desire. You are probably becoming a full-time artist for self-serving reasons but people don't hire you to glorify how great you are. They hire you because your work meets their current needs. It's not all about you.

It's about the benefits you provide. The goal is to create a demand for those benefits that YOU offer.

Now I know I have focused a great deal on the initial contact with people. That is extremely important. But what is equally important is being able to close the deal! If you can't get them to pay you, you can't survive. The sole purpose of why you want to be a full time artist is to follow your dreams. If you are not making money, that dream will quickly become a nightmare.

If you have a problem with asking people for money, you are not going to make a lot of sales. I believe what makes people fearful of asking for money is that they don't know if they are charging them too much. There are several ways to determine that:

You should try to find out what is the average amount of money artists at your career level are being paid. You can go with that number or you can try to do an Internet search on "How much should I charge for a performance gig?" or, "What is the average fee to hire a spoken word artist?"

You can't put the responsibility on the client by asking them how much is allotted in their budget for this service. Trust me, they are going to give you the lowest amount.

What do you think you should be paid? You may base that on the size of the audience, travel, meals, hotel, transportation, your performing time, your time waiting to perform, the time creating personalized or new pieces for this event.

You can start fairly high and negotiate the fee. You should have a minimum amount that you are not willing to accept less than and use that as your baseline.

You should never try to count the money in someone else's pocket if you can't see it. Ask for what you want. However, you have to be prepared to lose the gig.

Knowing the answer to these questions will make you more comfortable in asking for the money you deserve. On the other hand, you have to be able to outline why that cost is reasonable. You should be able to make the potential client comfortable. Ask questions about their event. Get as much information as you can. This will give you a visual of the event and will help you determine what to provide. You will also know what the client wants from you based on their response and your research, and then you should be able to say, "Ok. This is a breast cancer event. Well, my grandmother is a breast cancer survivor. I wrote a piece about how losing her breast crippled her self-esteem until she realized that her breast never defined her womanhood. She realized that she wasn't less beautiful but more uniquely gorgeous. And the best part of the piece is that she learned to smile and find her voice. She now shares her story of beauty, strength, and survival to other women in an effort to assist them in rescuing the beautiful woman that still lives inside of them." Being able to reassure the potential client that what you plan to deliver at their event will be outstanding and will benefit them and their audience. This reassurance will increase your chances of closing the deal. However, you can't successfully close a deal if you don't fully understand the needs of the client. Asking questions is the best way to get that information.

I recommend that you go to a bookstore or a library and retrieve some books on topics such as personal selling, thinking like a salesman, never over selling, meeting the needs of your customers, providing great customer service, the art of closing a sell, etc.

Please don't judge the book by its cover. Some of the best sales books that I have ever read were old and ugly. Base your purchasing decision on the insight of the author, table of contents, and the flow of the book. I don't care how bad I need to read a book, if I can't connect to the text it's not going to work. It always comes back to selling.

Trust me, reading these types of books will better assist you in achieving your goals as an artist.

Chapter 7

Creating Your Image

Your image is very important to your identity and your business. Your image consists of your style of dress, mannerisms, stage name, and your material. Your image is basically your trademark. Think of some of the big name hip-hop icons, computer moguls, and politicians that you are familiar with. Did a particular person come to mind when I just mentioned those titles? Did you immediately see their names, their style of dress, their mannerisms, their names, and the things they stand for or represent? This is what you want to happen when someone thinks of your art form. You want to be the identifying image that pops in their thoughts.

Your image should allow you to stand apart from others in your genre. If someone says, "You know the dude with the long dreads? He's slim and he does political poems." How many poets popped in your head? Now, what if they said, "You know the dude with the long dreads? He's slim, he recites political poems, and always gives one woman in the audience a rose." How many artists fit that description?

The goal is to always be remembered. Can someone describe you to the host of the venue you frequent where the host immediately knows that person being described is you? All they remember is your physical description and that you do political poems. If you are the only poet that does political poems in that venue, it should be easy for the host. However, if there are three other poets that do the same kind of poems, you could lose business because you are hard to find. So your image is crucial when you are a full time artist. Not being able to identify you could cost you money. I hear that change cup shaking.

Now there are pros and cons to having an image. A lot of artists try to avoid being branded because they feel it will limit their growth. However, if you are known for putting out quality products, then you will not be limited. Let's use the hip-hop mogul as an example. But take "mogul" off of his descriptor and just call him a hip-hop artist. Let's try to make him a mogul. He wears bulletproof vests, has a lot of tattoos, wears fitted sports caps, and is very controversial. Does that make him stand out? The bulletproof vest can, but if we know he has been shot nine times, that would help us identify him too.

Let's review his image. What does his image say to you? Stereotypically, his image could possibly say, aggressive African American male with ties to criminal activity. So one would possibly guess that he does gangster rap. For me, his image doesn't fit that genre. For his

millions of fans, it is the perfect image. His following
would be skeptical if he tried to sell an R&B album.
However, it wouldn't be farfetched if he appeared in a hood
film or a hood novel. Those things fit into HIS IMAGE.
This is also called typecasting. Many artists and actors hate
this.

The problem with typecasting and images is that
sponsors or investors are only comfortable with you doing
things that fit your type casted image. This is because
financial backers tend to believe your fan base will not
support you if you suddenly appear in a project that they
feel does not fit into their stereotypes of you. Sad, yet true.

How can this hip-hop artist broaden his
brand/image without losing his fan base? The first thing we
must understand is why would his fans feel he is limited? Is
it because this is all that they believe he is capable of?
Some do. It's easy for people to assume based on their own
stereotypes, biases, and limited information about you.
They may assume he is a good rapper. They may never take
into consideration that he is a businessman. My suggestion
to him would be to start building his fans' confidence in
him by releasing other artists who sell lots of CDs. The fans
will then think, "Hmmm. He has some business sense
because he can identify other talent and put them out on
HIS RECORD LABEL. The fan base will now have to
accept that he isn't as limited as they assumed. They may
still justify this business adventure as a good move because

it still fits within his image. My next suggestion would be
to appear in an action film that isn't classified as a ghetto
flick and with a love interest that isn't a ghetto chick. The
action parts of the film wouldn't be too farfetched because
the stereotypes suggest he has the potential to be violent.
The love interest will give him an opportunity to show a
loving and caring side towards a woman. If he does a great
job in the role, it would soften his appeal. He may even
pick up the gentle thug, which apparently appeals to a lot of
female fans. Now, he is a loving thug! I would then suggest
that he do a magazine interview on his business philosophy
and creating a legacy for his family. This would further
expand his base with people who have an understanding or
interest in business. By doing this, he would be connected
to people who care about the financial well being of their
future generations. Now his image has transformed into his
uniform and economical community he was born into.
People may begin to speak of him as a true success story,
which would make him more appealing and normal. My
next suggestion would be for him to be featured on a
Caucasian pop star single. This would show his crossover
appeal and further widen his base. He may not be singing
but he would be with a singer. His core group of fans may
start to see him a little different and become watchful to see
if he abandons them and crosses over with a new style of
music.

      Now how does this connect to you as an artist? I am
a spoken word artist with a very urban image. I usually
wear a du-rag and a black jacket. My image is considered

hood; an image to easily brand because there weren't many spoken word artists who were skinny, short, and look like they are in the process of committing a crime! To add, the majority of my material has an urban association. My fans began to expect this kind of material from me, which was great because it was easy to describe me. My work has hooks or choruses. There aren't too many spoken word artists with choruses. This allowed two ways to identify me and was excellent for my branding. However, the problem I faced was that my image made potential sponsors skeptical because I didn't fit their brand. I was too edgy. In other words, I was too scary. So, I took a similar approach as I suggested for the hip-hop artist. My new look is still urban in nature but with more of a crossover appeal. Subsequently, I started marketing my work toward organizations as a way to reach youth, ex-offenders, and people who struggle with the issues I incorporate in my performances. Using my new image along with my background and my ability to appeal to diverse audiences has created more opportunities for exposure and income. I started being hired as a subject matter expert, motivational speaker, and consultant. My personal background and my ability to transition into a businessman allowed them to identify me as a success story. I am no longer as scary looking. When I appear as my original image, people will see it as my uniform. The benefit for the smooth transition is that people aren't shocked to see me in a suit.

Let's look at another example: Two politicians. We will begin with the first one. Let's say his image is a man with good Christian values, which include family values, taking care of the elderly, and lowering taxes for the citizens of his country. Now let's say a woman accuses him of infidelity and he denies it. Time passes and he finally comes clean. His image is shattered and he gets voted out of office. His voters lost respect for him because they felt he lied and betrayed them. He could have been doing great things for his state. However, those good things are overshadowed because people believed he was a righteous man. Lets look at the other politician that has been accused of being a party animal and borderline delinquent in his youth. He is no longer that rambunctious child but he is now an outspoken and confrontational politician that is committed to fighting for the people of his state. One of his goals is better healthcare for the elderly and lowering taxes. He is also married and a Christian. Suddenly, while in office, a woman accuses him of infidelity. He denies it, and then later admits it happened. He would have a better chance of winning re-election because the voters were already aware of his playboy past. They may decide he has changed a lot by outlining the good he has done in office.

The differences between the two politicians are that one made the public believe he was perfect. The other politician's imperfections were known. Another difference to note is that the perfect politician hurt his voters because they believed he shared their same values. He was held up on pedestals as a role model. When he revealed his imperfections that made them feel betrayed and may have shattered their belief that a perfect person existed. The other politician is known to be a character capable of anything, but his intentions are good. So his lying wouldn't be farfetched but with his lowering taxes and helping the elderly in his state shows he followed through with his commitments to them.

My purpose for these examples is to warn you of the image you put out. If you are a goody two shoes, any dramatic and negative changes could potentially damage your reputation, career and your business, which damages your empire. In this case, it's easier to change from being bad to being good than vice versa.

Another thing to consider is your stage name. Please do not pick a stage name that too many other artists are already using. You should do an Internet search of the name to check if any artist is already using the name. Always try to be unique. The problem with having the same stage name is you can confuse your fans. The other artist can end up with opportunities that were meant for you. I don't want to hear, "What is meant for me is meant for me". In business, confusion leads to distrust and lost opportunities.

In addition, changing the spelling of your name doesn't help. If your stage name is Poetic RoachSpray, spelling it PoetixRoachSpray doesn't change how a person is going to say it. It will still be pronounced that same way. Also consider choosing a name that isn't too complicated to say because people will shorten it or call you something else. You don't want to choose a name like Poetic Pojabilocka and the host introduces you as "Poetic P!" People will rename you if they have too much trouble remembering how to say your name. On the other hand, you can teach people how to say it until they get it right.

Now if you are going to use your birth-name, make sure no one else has and is using the same name. If you find out that someone else is using your birth name, you can solve that problem by adding your middle initial or the whole middle name.

These are only suggestions. I want you to be true to you. This is a business and I want you to make money. Plus, you want to be marketable which means you want the opportunities to be abundant, whether you make them or they find you.

Chapter 8

Choosing Your Material

My deep brothers and sisters, I know your vocabulary is extraordinary. I love your fascination with words. I just want to warn you not to outsmart your audience. Chances are you will end up in front of more non-PhDs than those that have them. I am not saying don't use your vocabulary. I am forewarning you to know when to use it. Know your audience. I have found that when most people can't follow the depth of your pieces, they just say, "That was deep." Sometimes it is so deep that it goes over an audience's head. People hire folks they can connect to. Go as deep as you want to go but write some poems that first graders can understand. Now if your target markets are intellectuals only, then by all means, do your thang.

Please don't think I am trying to tell you what to write. There are millions of people who are very interested in whatever it is that you write. The task is that you have to be able to find those people. My goal is to encourage you to be all that you can be and assist you with a game plan on finding your audience. There are no limitations in life. Your potential is without boundaries.

I believe each piece that you write should have several components. These components are a plot with a beginning, a twist, a climax, and an ending. People love a good story. They will follow the story even if they try to tune it out. People expect to be told a story or the information may be hard to understand. Give them the basics of what they expect, but make sure you add a twist! People also expect to be shocked. Don't let them solve your story's ending before you get there. Don't be predictable. People love a good surprise.

So my friend, there are a few things that have lasted throughout time and those are roaches, prostitution, and stories. We know about the roaches and the prostitutes because someone wrote or told us a story about them! We even learn math in story form. Every song, commercial, conversation, movie, book and other forms of communication we receive are done in story form, so I think it would be wise if you follow that format.

Another thing I do is use hooks or choruses in 99% of my pieces. I know that children may not know a verse in their favorite song but they and even (non English speaking folks) can sing a chorus! So, yes… I follow the format of the music industry. My goal is to always be remembered. Now if someone heard me perform and they can't remember that my name is Lamont Carey, they usually say, "The little skinny dude with the du-rag, he has a poem that goes something like; "I can't read/ I can't write/ I can't spell/ and most of the time I don't know my left from my right". Their ability to remember certain things about me helps because there are enough clues to assist them in finding me. Also, an Internet search of my chorus can bring up information that leads to me as well. Making sure people can find you is extremely important! If folks can't find you, they can't hire you or purchase your product or other services. This is a part of marketing. Remember this: The goal is to always leave a trail so opportunities can find you!

Now I am not telling you what you should or shouldn't write or what to write about. You want to create your own identity. You want to be as unique as possible. This helps your work stand out as well. I am only making suggestions for you to consider. My next suggestion is that you should write about topics that you are passionate about. When you write about things that hurt and inspire you, your work will be more profound and impactful. Plus, it will be easier to write.

I think writing about what you know and care about is the best place to start. If you want to expand your topics, you can read about new stuff and/or experience them first hand. You need to be able to attach your essence to the new topics. Experiencing works better for me. The audience believes what you feel.

With a lot of new artists you can tell who their favorite artist is because they sound and perform just like that person. There is nothing wrong with using your favorite artist as inspiration to be creative. However, you should stay away from copying their style. The last thing you want at the beginning of your career is for people to say you are copying someone else's style. The word will spread and people will believe everything you do must belong to someone else. I know people say, "Don't trip off what others think." You should if this is the issue.

I was present in a venue when an artist performed another artist's work as if it was his own without giving credit to the original writer. I had no clue that it wasn't his work but the original writer was reciting every other stanza! The audience was quiet and looking back and forth. Then when the artist on stage finished, the originator of the work was called to the stage. He was a good sport. He announced that it was his work and that he told the guy to start giving him his credit. He did it all with a smile but the other guy finds it hard to get hired or even get on stages in their area because of this. Another issue for the infringer was missed opportunities. I was going to have him on a radio show that I was producing, but I couldn't have him on because I wasn't sure if he was going to recite his work or someone else's. My advice to you is, if you are going to recite someone else's work, give them credit at the beginning.

There is nothing wrong with studying your favorite artists and adapting techniques from their success to your plan. However, you should never try to be them. Inspire to be greater than them.

If you were an admirer of my work, I would hope that your thinking would be similar to this, "Okay, Lamont Carey wrote about the kid that they kept passing in school because he can play basketball really well but he can't read. I'ma write about the kid who is a superb student but has to be in a classroom with less performing kids because of the No Child Left Behind Act." The focuses of the pieces are still on the school system and students but the approach is entirely different and both are relevant.

I further suggest that you think about which artists you like and why. Do these artists appeal to you because of their unique image, their material, their performance style or a combination of all three? Think about why other artists don't keep your attention. Try to understand as much as you can about both sets of performers. How similar are they to you and your work? Do you like them because they write about things you care about? What kind of audience was there and how did they respond to them? Was the audience clapping for them just because the host told them to or did they genuinely love the artist's work? Think about their body of work. Are most of their pieces on relationships? Politics? Slavery? Inner-city life? Revolution? Studying the performers and the audiences at these venues will help you understand how to connect to a crowd. You incorporate what works into your already unique presentation style. It's all about emotionally connecting to your audience.

Remember you are not mimicking the other artists' style. You are learning how they are capturing, holding and turning audiences into fans.

Chapter 9

Mastering The Stage

First of all, writing for the page and writing for the stage are two different forms of writing. You can be an amazing book writer but you can suck as a performer. If you plan to just release books and never perform then you are fine. However, if you plan to recite in front of audiences, you will have to practice performing your work to figure out where you need to make changes. I am not saying that you have to rewrite your whole piece…simply recite it. You can literally feel where your flow becomes clumsy or when it doesn't sound right in your ears. You have to trust what you hear and feel. If you hear it, your audience will feel it too. You can keep the theme and story of your piece but you may have to alter or exchange some of the words to make reciting your piece flow with the rhythm you desire.

As a full time artist, you should focus as much time on developing your performance as you do on your writing style. The two go hand in hand. The audience comes to hear heartfelt words and to be entertained. It is your responsibility to leave them with an everlasting experience. Those are the same people who will hire you. They won't come looking for you if you don't leave your performance engraved in their memories. The goal is to make an impression with your words and your stage performance. If you do a great job with that, you will stand out.

In order to do a great job, the audience has to hear every word you say. If the audience has any trouble hearing more than a few words, they may tune your entire performance out. You don't want that to happen. You want to captivate them and hold their attention until you are done. I suggest that you always perform the material that you love or the one that has gotten the best reactions out of audiences.

Another thing that you should pay attention to is reading or knowing your audience. It is difficult to explain but you may have experienced that you shouldn't cuss when you are performing in front of elementary school students. They will laugh but the principal and teachers won't like you very much. You probably shouldn't do erotic poems in churches either or gay-bashing poems at a gay pride event. This is what I mean by reading or knowing your audience. Professionals will know what to say and what not to say in front of specific audiences. Learn your audience.

I also strongly suggest that you practice projecting your voice to the back of the room. I have experienced a microphone dying many times or the sound system is terrible. I know in many small venues there aren't any microphones at all so you should be prepared to project your voice around that room like a true professional does. The show must go on.

Now take a few seconds to think about what made you fall in love with your artistry. Did you fall in love because you believed all of the artists you saw were horrible and you felt you could do a better job? Or were there some artists that completely amazed you? Was it their words, stage presence, or both? Once you figure out what captivated you about this art form, then you will know how your audience should feel during your performance.

When you are rehearsing your pieces, do you see yourself performing in front of huge crowds on a world-class stage with great lighting and all the things a superstar needs in that moment? Me too! It is your responsibility to mentally perform every piece on that stage…every time. I don't care how many times you perform. You should bring that same level of passion and professionalism. It's your job to make the audience as emotionally connected to you and your work, as you were when you created it. No matter the size of the audience.

In addition, I want you to get off that paper! You are a professional artist. You should not walk on stage reading from any paper. You should be performing from memory. The main issue I have with reading from paper is that it can easily disconnect you from the audience. It is hard to look into the eyes of an audience member and see that they are in tune with you. It's hard to add emotions to your work if you are worried about skipping a line.

Again, think about your favorite artist: What do you love about them? If your favorite artist is a poet whose books you have read, have you ever seen them perform live? Is it as powerful being read aloud? Now think about the venues you have been to and saw poets read from paper verses artists who perform from memory. Are both equally powerful on that stage? How many singers or rappers do you know come on stage and perform while reading their lines from paper?

You want the audience to be drawn into your world. You want your voice to be passionate and full of emotions. When you reach those lines where you felt sad, the audience should feel the same pain. When you reach that point where you're smiling or laughing, the audience should be experiencing the same thing. There is no other way to get them there unless you emotionally become a part of the performance piece.

It is said that the mark of a true professional performer is that they always come prepared to perform and never stop performing regardless of what is going on around them. People can be screaming, breaking glass, cussing you out but you're not supposed to stop performing. I agree. The only time you should stop performing is when your life is in danger. I can't tell you when that is. You would have to decide when you're scared of the threat of bodily harm or death.

Another thing you should never do is stopping a performance to tell the audience you forgot your lines. They won't know if you don't tell them. Here are some ways to handle a situation when you forget a line: (1) You can repeat the lines before several times with inferences on the words while you search your brain for the missing line or do a dramatic pause. Say your last line was, "She screamed at me!" I would hold my ears with my eyes closed tightly. DRAMATIC effect. I have no idea what it means but let the audience try figuring it out because they will believe it is part of the performance! (2) You can softly repeat the lines like I was hurting or torn because of her screaming at me. Once the line is retrieved, I would keep on performing like nothing ever happened. (3) You should also learn how to do improvisation (improv) just in case the line never comes back. You can keep on with your performance and end it without saying, "Dang. I forgot the poem. Let me do another one." Learning improvisation will increase your confidence with your stage performance.

Don't forget you are your talent and Your Art Is Your Empire. Most spoken word artists don't have tracks

to play. They don't need a sound check. They don't need a
dress rehearsal. All you need for the host to do is say,
"You're on". That's when your magic happens. For artists
that need to do sound checks, listen to the quality of the
sound system because that is what the audience will hear.
This is your night. This is your opportunity. You are the
star so get the sound quality as great as it can be.

Chapter 10

Don't Leave Home without THESE Items

Ok. You've decided to be a full time artist. You have your plan in order. Your taxes and copyrights are covered. You're confident in your ability to sell yourself and your image is solid. Now you are ready to go light up the venues with your stage performance. HOLD UP. There are three things I feel you should never leave the house without… at anytime; your cellular phone, your business cards, and some of your memorized material or art. Four things if you are a musical act. You should have some of your best musical tracks on hand.

As a full time artist, your business is your artistry. You should never find yourself in a situation where someone requests to hear a sample of your work and you reply, "I didn't bring anything with me." You should be able to recite a poem, spit a rhyme, or show a canvas of your art at a moments notice. You never know where or what situation you will find yourself in. You could end up at a location and someone wants to hire you on the spot to perform in minutes! It has happened to me several times and I was prepared to take that money off of their hands and increase my brand. That also builds their confidence in me being able to deliver. Plus, you never know whom you will meet. You could find yourself face to face with a promoter, television executive, an agent, a tour manager, etc. These folks may request to hear a sample of what you can do. Being able to recite immediately gives you an advantage over an artist that hands out CDs every day. They get to hear you at that moment. Then you can hand them a business card.

A business card is extremely important for full time artists because you are never off of the work clock. Your job is 24/7; therefore, you need to always have a business card. In this day and time, writing your number down on a piece of paper doesn't look professional! Business should never be conducted like you are out on the dating scene and you just met somebody. Potential clients expect you to be professional. A business card gives the impression that you are professional and prepared to conduct business.

I believe your business card should stand out from everyone else's. The best way to make your card stand out is to have your card say everything you want to say about you. You also should have your picture on it. Most business people are handed business cards often so when they are revisiting and skimming through their collection of cards, you want your card to stand out. Here are some of the ways I try to stand out:

I have a clear picture of my face on the front and back of the card. This is effective because that person will immediately recognize me. This will remind them of our conversation and why they were given my card. I want my picture on both sides because most people don't have anything on the back of their card and especially not a picture of themselves. More importantly, I want my picture on the cards so I can continue to brand my image in order for people to associate my face with my art form. You remember in the previous chapter where I named the politician, hip-hop mogul, and computer mogul? Remember I said that you want your image to pop in the person's head when they hear that title. This further helps with branding your image with your art form.

My work title and services that I offer are on the front side of the card. This is to help trigger the memory of the person that rediscovers my card months later. I may look familiar to them but they don't recall our conversation. Having the services that I offer reminds them that I am an artist and the art form I specialize in.

My contact number is on the business card. This number should never be shut off or changed. I will pay my phone bill over any other bill because my phone is one of the main tools that I use to make money. If a person can't reach me by phone, I can't make money. My art form is my income so I have to always have my phone operating. This should be the one thing in your life that doesn't change.

You can have another number but your business number must remain the same for life. Some people may not call you until years later but you don't want to lose a moneymaking opportunity because you changed your number. Please if you can afford another line to handle your personal calls, do so! You can change your personal number as much as you want but your business phone should never be changed!!! To add, your business phone should be a cell phone in my opinion. I want to be accessible. I know some people say you should appear busy and don't call people right back! I don't agree with that. If I were that busy, I would have a secretary taking my calls. For example, let's say your contact number is a house or office phone. You're not at work and a popular art show calls but no one answers. Bare in mind that they have a list of artists they are interested in booking on the show this season. When no one answers your phone, chances are they are going to keep going down their list. They are on a timeline. You just missed a major opportunity to be broadcast worldwide. This situation can also happen on a much smaller scale. Most people that are hiring artists to perform are making calls in the planning stages. Time is money for them and you. Make yourself available. When you can afford to have a secretary or a booking agent take your calls, then you don't have to answer your phone. Then again, you should always have your number available. I have several agents, managers and other kinds of booking folks I work with or have worked with. These relationships end for whatever reason. Now if you all end on bad terms and someone calls to book you for an event, this person might just say, "We don't work together anymore," and hang up the phone. You just missed an opportunity to make money! You can have a voice mail setup so your calls go straight to it but you should check your voicemail EVERYDAY! PLEASE. PLEASE PLEASE DO NOT have any LOUD, STATIC filled, cursing music or people talking on your voicemail. Don't create one of those voice messages that fool people into believing you are on the phone only to have you say, "Got-Cha!" I would be like, "I got'cha all right. I'm moving on to the next person. The jokes are on you". Remember, Your Art Is Your Empire. You are a business professional. Your voice message and call waiting should be clear and tell people to leave their name, number, and a brief message. Advise them on how to contact you if it is an emergency. Now if you lose your cell phone/business phone or it is stolen, you should immediately obtain a back up phone and have your phone company switch your service to this phone until your replacement phone comes. Another option is to change your voicemail through the phone company to tell people to call you at another number until your phone situation is corrected. You should always keep a copy of your contacts just in case something happens to your phone. Keep a back up phone somewhere. Stay accessible in order to stay in business.

You should also have an email address on your business card. This email address should ALWAYS be active. Again some folks will not seek you out for months or years later but you want them to be able to still contact you. Some people prefer to email you instead of calling you, so you want to give them that option.

Your brand should be visible even through the card. If you have a logo, that logo should be visible on the card. You want people to be able to see your logo and immediately know it is you. Think of some of the household names of restaurants, car companies, entertainment, and clothing logos that you identify with and know exactly what they do. You want to create that for yourself. You are working 24/7 even if you are not physically there.

Have a short version of your bio on the back of your standard size business card. You should have the most recognizable venue names of the places you have performed or featured included in that brief bio. Now if you have only performed at major events, you should list the top three that will appeal to people in your target market and those that you don't usually target. This will help you sell yourself better. Try using the familiar names and popular places that are associated with your art form. I use some that my target audience recognize and others that would surprise a different demographic to see that I have performed there. My goal is to inform my target market and expand it. Imagine how impressive someone who wouldn't come to see you perform discovers on your business card that you have performed at the WHITE HOUSE. This could create new money making opportunities for you.

People are impressed with places and events that they deem successful. They love introducing new things to their friends, family, and colleagues. Use your success to make you more successful.

    Always leave a trail for people to find you. Your business card is a great tool to lead them to you. If you don't have a business card, a professional flyer will suffice. Just make sure the flyer has all of the important information on it.

Chapter 11

Your First Product

We have covered a great deal of your business needs. Now let's walk out of the door prepared to sell some products and services. I am going to assume that you are starting off with only your written material. To add, you have very little money. Now the least expensive and easiest product to create is a copy of one (or a few copies) of your work. The first thing you need is to have the written material typed. Once that happens the name changes officially to lyric sheets but you can keep it simple and call it poems or lyrics.

You want to have your work printed double sided on one piece of paper. Since you will be printing your lyrics on 8-1/2 by 11 paper, you can format the layout in two or three columns on the front. You just want the font to be big enough to be read easily. I usually use the standard font size of 12 or bigger when using one column. Now when you are trying to fit it all on the front page, you shouldn't go lower than 11 in font size. This may mean that the text has to go on the back of the paper. The problem that I have with putting it on the back of the paper is that the buyer can't hang it up in their house. We want as many people to see your work as possible. However, if all the text doesn't look right on the front page, you have to put some of the lyrics on back of the page. I prefer it to look good on both sides than to have it all on the front and not be legible.

Having your poem on two or more pieces of paper makes it difficult for the purchaser to carry, display or show off to others. You want the buyer to be able to show the sheets off to others. Most people shy away from reading three pages of something, yet they will read one page. You should always want the buyer to have a pleasant memory of purchasing from you. You don't want them to have to figure out where to store your work. When most people make a purchase they have an idea of where they are going to keep it in their home. Are you like that? We don't want them struggling to carry these different prints of your one poem so lets try to make it easy for them. One way is to supply them with a bag that has a handle. However, this will increase your cost in production because you have to purchase the bag, which maybe worth it. If your money doesn't agree, stick with the one sheet.

At this point, you don't need one hundred copies! You'll need maybe ten copies of the poems you are going to perform. Choose two of your best pieces or two that audiences generally like. You can have them printed on regular paper or on some fancy designed paper of your choosing. The only suggestion that I will make about printing your work on pretty craft paper is that you have to make sure it doesn't overshadow your written work. This basically means don't use any designed paper that makes it difficult to read. If someone has to struggle to read one word, that's a problem. They are paying for the poem, not the design. Please do not try to sell any of your work with graphics that look cheap or faded.

Once it is typed, find someone or a copier that can laminate the material. You want to laminate it so that it lasts longer. Make sure you put the copyright logo and the year at the bottom of the poem as well. So folks know it is protected. Another thing that should be present is your name, email, and website address. Whoever lays eyes on the sheet can see your contact information should they want a copy or want to reach out for a potential opportunity. I didn't always do this. I'm sure I missed many opportunities to sell more copies, perform live, or make myself available for other possibilities.

Be mindful that I don't want you to make things look cluttered, so if you can only put the copyright logo, your name, and website on it, that's fine. You just want people to be able to find you. If you can't always afford to have your website up and running, then put your email address on it instead.

You now have your first product. You have to determine what price you should sell it for. I believe the average cost is around $5 to $6. I would choose $5 quicker than I would choose $6 because people tend to have $5 bills. They would hate to have to make change of a bigger bill just to give you $1. Convenience is good. Some people sell sheets for waaaaaaaaaaaaay more than that. I just want you to consider the kind of money transferring hands in the venue you are going to. If you are going to an OPEN MIC venue, chances are the average cost for food is $5 and the average cost to get in is $5 therefore people will more than likely have a few $5 bills in their pockets. Your job is to own one of those $5 bills!

Being able to accept payments electronically will be a good way to increase your sells. Obtaining a credit card swiper is another good idea. Not many people are carrying around cash but they do have a credit/debit card. You can find companies' online, retail stores and banks that offer credit card swipers. They are easy to use.

Chapter 12

Building Your Resume

This is one of the most crucial steps in your efforts to making more money as an artist. I know when I wanted to start making money; I was told that I had to start doing free gigs to get my name out there before I was "WORTHY" of being paid. I was told that by artists who didn't have a clue as to how to get paid or wanted to keep me away from the money they were trying to make. I don't want that for you. I want you to make as much money as you can.

There are several ways to get your name buzzing but that doesn't mean it will instantly lead to the amounts of money you will need to live comfortably from your craft. Below are some of the ways I know artists have used to get their name out to the masses:

OPEN MICS

An Open Mics (open microphone) is the generic name for places where new artists go to perform and art lovers gather to experience art in its rawest form. Open Mics are usually small events held inside of cafes, restaurants, houses, coffee houses, and art galleries that can accommodate fifty people or less. Open Mics are popular in most major cities around the world. They're always open to the public. Typically, you'll sign your name on a list to perform. No other requirement is necessary. When the host calls your name, you go to the stage or performing area and recite one to two pieces of your material. Generally, Open Mics do not pay the performers. Some venues charge an entry fee.

Some Open Mics do pay their FEATURED artists to perform and the pay varies. The featured artist is considered the STAR of the night and will generally perform up to twenty minutes or three to four pieces of their work. Getting a feature spot isn't always easy. This is reserved for artists who are popular and/or have an established fan base that will come out to see the artists perform. They also may be friends of the host. Sometimes, you find a great host who wants to give a newcomer with potential an opportunity to feature.

You can do an Internet search of "open mic" or "poetry venues" in your state or city. Always call before you go because Open Mics disappear a lot but one is always opening at another location.

Hosting an Open Mic can generate you a little consistent money. Some hosts have grown their audience to the point that they have companies and individuals sponsoring their events, which helps pay the host as well as the feature. Hosting open mics helps with keeping your name in front of the poetry community.

Open Mics are great when starting off. You can try out new pieces and receive constructive feedback from audiences or seasoned artists. They're also a good place to start building your fan base, finding out where the other open mic venues are, and structuring your stage presence to make a name for yourself in your area.

As you start making more money to perform outside of Open Mics, you have to take some precautions. I would limit how often or eliminate featuring at Open Mics because it can effect how much you get paid. Let's say you are getting paid $500 or more to perform outside of Open Mics. Someone with money to pay your commanding amount ends up at an Open Mic for whatever reason. You just finished your feature and you are talking to your fans after the show. The person who can pay you what you are currently worth wants to talk to you, but you're still engaging with fans. This person goes to the host and brags about how much he loves your work then asks the host how much it costs to get you to perform. The host says, "$50". This person then approaches you after your fans release you. He tells you about the event they're hosting and offers you $50 when their original offering price was probably $2000. Most businesses will never disclose what they were willing to pay especially if they can hire you for less. You may find out if another artist is also doing the event and unknowingly admits it to you. You will be pissed with the person who hired you and you may feel that they robbed you, however, they were only paying you what they learned you were currently getting paid at the Open Mic.

My suggestion is to continue attending Open Mics on occasion. When you do attend, sign up as an Open Mic'er (performer). You can still promote, build your following, support the venue, and allow potential clients to see you perform. This is just my opinion.

I love Open Mics but I have experienced at least three of those situations. I will say that if you are just starting out on your own and you can get a spot as a feature, do it. If someone offers you $50 and you aren't making anything, get that $50. For the moment you are now worth $50.

FESTIVALS

Festivals tend to attract hundreds or even thousands of people to an event. This can be good for you because it allows people to experience your work that may never go to an Open Mic. The other benefit is that it attracts a lot of businesses that could become interested in hiring you to perform at one of their functions. These could lead to larger paying gigs.

Another plus for performing at festivals, the pay is usually more than Open Mics. The challenge with festivals is that people are constantly walking around, trying to see all and hear all. They are not stationed. However, if your stage presence is commanding, you can attract a crowd to you.

To find upcoming festivals, you can do a search on the Internet, visit various galleries, cafes, and check your local classified sections of newspapers. Contact information is usually available such as a phone number or website. If there is a website in the listing, check the website for submission information. If there is not a website but there is a number, I would call them and ask if they are still accepting submissions for the festival. If not, ask when is the next one, and when do they start selecting artists. Let them know you want to send your bio or press kit to their email. It is always great to call them early.

One of the advantages in becoming associated with festivals early is so the promoters can have your picture, email, bio, and contact information on their website. You will be amazed at how many people contact you from their sites either before or after the festival if they enjoyed you. If booked, you'll get to network with various artists of different genres as well as festival staff. Additionally, the staff usually freelances at other events where they can possibly suggest that the producers check you out. NETWORK. NETWORK. Again, the drawback is getting those people to stop and pay attention. Nothing is impossible. I've done it.

POETRY SLAMS

Most new artists try to become popular by competing in slams as individuals. If you are into slamming, this can be great for you. You can get your name out there and you can win awards or whatever prizes are offered. Slam poets tend to travel the country to compete in slams, which are a great way to meet other poets, promoters, fans of spoken word, and to build your name. Spoken word artists even join "slam teams" where they compete against other slam teams.

4. SHOWCASES

There are tons of showcases going on all around the country from TV shows to community events. Showcases are great because you can network with other artists, win awards, build your fan-base, get interviewed by blogs and newspapers, and find booking agents and managers. Some showcases have a registration fee.

5. CONTACTS

Every family member, friend, neighbor and associate you have that works in the private, public, and underground world can help you build your resume. Some of these individuals are capable of arranging opportunities for you to showcase your talents to a wide range of people who can move your career forward and help you build your fan base. These individuals may be more than willing to assist you if you ask. If your Aunt works at Showtime, see if she can arrange for you to perform at a conference or anything where there may be power players in the room. The goal is to get those executives to see you and come up with ways you can benefit their next venture. If you are only able to perform that one time you can still list on your resume that you performed for Showtime. Too often new artists look outside of their contacts to find new people to open doors that are already accessible to you. Reroute your thinking. Who do you know that can help you get a gig? It can be a friend, a friend of a friend, or anyone. Think strategically. These people will have close relationships with other folks who can secure an opportunity for you to perform.

All of this is a process so don't get discouraged. There are too many people in this world who regret not living their dreams. That doesn't have to be you. Being a full time artist is not going to be easy. You will have a lot of moments where you become frustrated. You will have a whole lot of experiences where your material will change not only your life but also the lives of others. No one can get your message across better than you. No one.

You're going to have a whole lot of naysayers and haters who will tell you this is a waste of time and money. In those moments remember you're accomplishments. Ask them if The White House has ever contacted them to perform. Ask them have they ever had a letter written to them from children and adults around the world telling them how their material helped them in someway. Ask them do they have any licensing agreements with another country. Ask them have they appeared on any television program as a guest. Ask them if they are living their dreams. All of this is possible for you and more because I have done it. There is nothing more special about me than there is for you. You can truly become whatever you want to become but you're going to have to work hard to make it a reality. You're going to face some hardships but you will accomplish so much on your journey. When it gets really rough, stop and look at those accomplishments to see if they motivate you to keep going.

Also remember that you can always walk away from your dream if it becomes too much of a burden. A lot of people only see the dream and not understand that this is a business. To fulfill your dream you have to take care of the business side or you'll end up broke and broken. If you don't give yourself a chance to accomplish your dreams, you may regret it for the rest of your life. I want you to be

84

happy. If becoming a professional artist is your dream,
learn everything about the reality of your dream. Study
folks who are or have lived it. Become aware of their
hurdles and how they overcame them. Then create a plan.
Remember the things I mentioned in this book.

Chapter 13

What Is a Bio & How To Write One

Bio is the abbreviation for biography. It is similar to a resume. Both are used to sell your expertise. The difference is that in this context, a Bio gives the reader a glimpse into your work as an artist. The bio is written like a school essay with an opening, a body, and a closing. The bio is basically you bragging about what you have accomplished without seeming like you're bragging. You know folks want you to be humble. *Laughing. *

You should have at least two bios: a long version and a short version. The long one will be more detailed with information about your personal life and your life as an artist. It will include where you were born and raised. It will include degrees if you have any. I wouldn't say I graduated from such and such high school unless you are submitting this bio to that school to give you an upper hand on getting the gig. The reason I wouldn't mention that you graduated from a school and didn't go to a college because it brings attention to what you haven't done. I would focus on the pluses. You don't want to be in the process of a school considering hiring you as a potential motivational speaker for students and you haven't graduated.

At times, your delinquent past will become relevant. For instance, you were a kid that stayed in trouble but turned your life around as an adult. This information could be relevant when you are speaking to the students, specifically at-risk students. A past filled with bad choices, wrong crowds and foolishness can be used as a testament to help in improving one's future. Either way, it is your choice on whether you mention you didn't finish school. I wouldn't unless it was relevant to the gig.

Now people love to know where you were born and raised, especially if you come from their state. You're like a local hero. People love talking to someone about things they may have in common. You can use this information in your talks to further build a connection with your audience if you mention areas they would be familiar with.

You would also want to include your biggest life accomplishments in the arts. If you started a company, that's a plus. If you have performed for a well-respected politician or at a landmark building, that's a plus. If you have performed with other well-known artists, that's a plus. If you have received any awards, that's another plus. Remember the goal of the bio is to sell you as an expert in your field or someone with experience.

You can also write about the impact your work has on your audiences. If you spoke at a church and someone decided to give their life to God because of you, I think saving souls is newsworthy. If you spoke to a group of at-risk kids and one decided to change their life that's newsworthy. You get my point.

In my opinion, the longer bio should be no longer than a page. You can include as many major accomplishments as you would like, and should the longer bio on your website via the ABOUT ME page. The same bio should appear on your social media pages and your press kit.

The shorter bio should be about a paragraph long. You may have to limit your focus to your biggest accomplishments: awards, your company's name, biggest places you have been featured, etc. The shorter bio can be read before your showcase and go on the back of your business card, news articles, fliers or where it would fit within limited spaces.

Since I am one of those people who has to see stuff in order to make sure I am using the right format, I am including my long and short bio for your reference…

LONG BIOGRAHY:

In 2010, Mr. Carey embarked upon his career as a playwright and producer with two plays "Laws Of The Street" (a play he is currently developing into a TV series) and "Learning To Be A Mommy" both of which were performed at John F. Kennedy Center's Terrace Theatre in Washington, D.C. In addition to the TV series, Mr. Carey is also producing and directing a powerful documentary detailing the successful transition of four ex-offenders; a story with personal meaning to Mr. Carey.

Mr. Carey is a dynamic motivational speaker and workshop facilitator for youth and adults alike. His ability to encourage and invoke change has been experienced locally as well as in states such as Texas, Atlanta and New York. He has been invited by various government officials and community leaders to host or speak at a number of events which includes the Office of Returning Citizen's Affairs' annual Returning Citizens Community Appreciation Day and Congresswoman Eleanor Holmes Norton's Commission on Black Men and Boys hearing which addressed the topic, Project Graduation– First Steps to Success for Young Black Men in the District of Columbia Conquering High Dropout Rates. Mr. Carey has also been a guest speaker at graduations and opening ceremonies for organizations such as Operation Hope, Court Services and Offender Supervision Agency (CSOSA) and W.C. Smith and Company.

Mr. Carey's heart for the community, in particular African-American boys who may be facing some of the challenges he experienced growing up, led him to recently develop the program Raise A Man™. The purpose of the program is to connect African American boys with productive programs that are operated or facilitated by African American men.

Mr. Carey has received numerous awards including the first U.S. Parole Commission's Re-Entry and Service Award in 2012 and the One Degree of Separation Re-entry Community Service Award, Senate Congressional Award in 2008, Congressional Achievement Award, The Good Black Man Award, National Underground Spoken Word and Poetry Awards (NUSPA) in 2007 and Poet of the Year award in 2005.

SHORT BIOGRAPHY

Lamont Carey is an internationally known spoken word artist, motivational speaker, workshop facilitator, filmmaker, playwright, and author.

He has appeared on HBO's Def Poetry Jam and The Wire, B.E.T's Lyric Cafe and various radio shows including the Michael Basiden Show. He is also the Director of his TV series Laws Of The STREET, and other independent film projects.

Bam! They are the same but one just has more details. I personally like the smaller one but some places love to read that long one. So create both so you can use the one that fits the situation.

Chapter 14

The Barter System

I thought this chapter was relevant because most new artists don't have enough money to pay for all of the services they need. So, if you are good at a task like promoting, singing, writing, or anything you may do extremely well, you may be able to barter with someone who has something you need.

Bartering is the exchange of products or services without using money. It's an exchange of products and services in return for other products or services between two parties, minus the monetary transactions. For examples: You want to apply for a small artists grant to teach vocal lessons but you don't have any space to hold the classes. You could probably approach a recreation center and ask them to allow you to use a room and in return you will give a selected number of the kids who hang out at the recreation center free vocal lessons. Bartering.

Another example of this is: If you'll make this logo for me, I'll promote your company through my website. Bartering.

If you are good at something, you may be able to barter with someone else. One last example for you: You are trying to shoot a short film. You can advertise online or get the word out that you are looking to cast some non-union actors in your film. In return for payment, you provide the actors with a scene from the film to use in their portfolio or offer to shoot a monologue of them. Bartering.

Be mindful that there are millions of new artists, new businesses and people in general who need what you can offer and have what you need. You just have to find each other. I would suggest you make your wants known everywhere from colleges, to retirees to your social media. Everywhere. Just state what you want and what you will offer in return.

Lastly, colleges are always great places to barter. You have students learning all of these new and exciting things and finding exciting ways to do old things. Some can't wait to test their skills in the real world. If they can make it a school assignment, they will typically get a grade or some type of credit for it. Bartering.

Chapter 15

Paying Yourself

One of the biggest mistakes I think new artists make is not paying themselves. We will pay for the studio time, the CD duplication, the photographer, the business cards and everything else. Everyone else gets paid but ourselves. A sure way for your company to grow is to re-invest, which is awesome, but you have to pay yourself. You need to create a separation from you and your business. If you don't separate the two they will always be one. You'll find yourself paying personal bills and excursions with what could have been set aside for business or you'll use funds for business and never have any money for yourself. You have to know where your personal life begins and your business begins and vice versa.

I suggest you look at your business as your management company. What percentage are you willing to pay a manager to represent you? You can pay the business anywhere from ten to thirty-five percent of your gross income from all of your gigs. This means your management company wants to get paid just like the IRS. They want their percentage from the $50 you made at the open mic. They don't want their percentage of the money left over after you grab you something to eat and put some gas in the car. The gas and the food can be listed as a business expense but you would have to work that out with your accountant. So, lets go back to the gas and food you purchased. You spent $10 on the food and you put $10 in the gas tank and say that was a business expense, right? You're paying your management 50% of what you made tonight. I would love to be your manager because that is awesome for management but crazy for the artist! Lets look at this with a business eye. If you pay your management 10% of your gig, that's $5 going back into the business and you will be left with $45. Don't forget the taxes you have to pay so that $45 isn't completely yours yet.

You tell yourself that $5 is not a lot of money to re-invest back into the business. You decide to up the percentage to 20%. You pay 10% to the company and another 10% to your management. You just invested $10 back into the business. You also realize that you have to pay Uncle Sam his $4 (8%). You now have $36 to splurge with! Now you can buy your gas and eat your meal in peace and still be in business.

If you are asking why I added the extra $5 for business, my reason is that because I know you wouldn't feel right putting only $5 back into your business. Remember, you are building an empire. To make you feel better, we can look at the $5 for management fee as getting yourself comfortable for when you acquire someone who

manages artists for a living. For now you are doing a great
job at it.

In any case, the point I was trying to make is that
you separate yourself from your business. You should draw
a line. Now $10 doesn't buy you a whole lot of studio time
but you can always lend your company some money and
expect to be paid back.

Chapter 16

The Beauty of Banking

I am not a financial advisor. I am a professional and full time artist. I am only sharing my experiences and what I had to do to prepare, protect, organize, build, and grow my business.

Before I started trying to separate what I needed to pay Uncle Sam, LaCarey Enterprises, LLC, I used to put my money in a dresser drawer next to my bed. I have always been devoted to paying cash for what I needed for the business. I just never paid myself. Well, yes I did. When I needed something like carryout food or clothes, I would just go into the drawer and pay for it. The problem with that was that I was spending the IRS money, LaCarey Enterprises, LLC money, and my money. I did not know I owed all these people even though two of them were me. However, at the end of the year when I had to see Uncle Sam, I couldn't always remember everything, especially when some of my business receipts faded from being in my back pocket after a few days. I am one of those people who transfer everything from one pair of pants to the next without really thinking about it.

Long story short, I had to start separating my money after I couldn't prove to Uncle Sam how much I really made and what my expenses were. Uncle Sam said that I owed him way more than I could possibly owe and he MADE me pay him. In order to avoid that again, I needed to start operating like a real businessman. I started thinking about opening a bank account. Now you have to remember, I like holding my money. I like balling up my money. I like to see those presidents wave and popping out at me when I play with my money. Thinking about putting my money in a bank's hands was not easy. I started thinking about their issues. You know, bank fraud, bank robbery, check fraud, embezzlement, bankruptcy, closing at a certain time of the day and not opening on certain days, etc. I thought those people had too many issues that they needed to work out before I could trust them. I made my final decision and opened two bank accounts, a personal account and a business account for LaCarey Enterprises, LLC.

Anyway, I decided to go to the first bank I saw and talk to someone there. I talked to a bank manager. She told me that I would need my business license, an Employer Identification Number (EIN), identification and a deposit to open a business bank account. She proceeded to tell me that I just needed a government issued identification to open a personal account and that my money would be federally insured at the bank. Basically, if something went wrong the government would pay me my money up to $100,000. Hearing that made me feel at ease because I didn't have a $100, 000 to give anybody!

She made me feel so comfortable that night, I kissed my presidents good night and told them that I will miss them but I promise to visit often and take them out from time to time. I then gathered my business paperwork and opened a bank account for LaCarey Enterprises, LLC and a personal account, so I could separate the money, which was a good thing. I felt legit. I felt successful. This also made me more aware of money because most of my checks were signed to LaCarey Enterprises, LLC. I had to know when they cleared so I could get paid. Once the checks cleared, I would go into the bank and have them transfer my pay out of the business account.

The nice lady at the bank told me that this wasn't a good way to show what the money was withdrawn for. She asked me if I knew how to write checks. I didn't so she taught me. She then ordered me some checks and asked about my credit. I didn't have any so she talked to me about debit cards; secure credit cards, and credit cards.

I eventually chose a debit card, which looked like a credit card but I when used it, money was taken immediately out of my bank account. To me, it was like using actual cash without using cash. Well, it was still cash, but the card was my cash. I liked that because I was uncomfortable owing anyone. Additionally, I am a full-time artist and my gigs weren't consistent enough where I felt secure in being able to pay back the bank.

Once my gigs became more consistent I opted for a secure credit card. The secure credit card basically meant that I was allowing the bank to put a hold on $99 of my money. They would then give me another card that looked like a credit card. I would spend the $99 on this card and pay a percentage back every month. A hold would be placed on the card if I failed to pay the money back, but the bank already has my money to take what is owed. I did this for about six months and paid the monthly note. After the six months period, they released my $99 back to me. My secure card turned into a credit card with a limit of $500 dollars. The bank now trusts that I will pay them back so they increased my balance; hence I was using their money. I liked using their money! Through this process, I developed good credit score.

I moved from having my money in the dresser drawer to having a credit card and establishing a credit score history. In addition, I am now writing checks when I purchase products and services for my business. This made me feel awesome. It changed how I looked at the money or checks I received. I automatically knew I had to deposit the check because it was in the company's name, wait for the check to clear, and then write a check from the company to myself for my fee. I was also paying the IRS every month. I was feeling more and more professional.

I was soon ready to take on the ATM. The bank manager told me how to use it but I didn't want to know my password and still don' know it. I felt I would take money out too easily. I wanted to wait to go in to the bank. I went from being uncomfortable with depositing my money in the bank to being uncomfortable withdrawing it.

I later spoke with the bank manager about opening a Revolving Line of Credit for my business. She saw that I had been paying more than my monthly balance on the credit card so she typed in some information based on questions she asked and submitted a request for a line of credit. It was approved! The line of credit was simply a bank loan where the bank loaned me a certain amount of money for my business. My balance had been increased from $0 to $99 to $500 to $4,000. It felt good to be growing my financial resources. All I had to do was pay the minimum monthly balance (and interest of course) and the bank would continue to support my efforts.

This may be something you can use to your benefit. I went in to get help separating my personal income from my business gigs. I ended up creating a relationship with a bank that helped me build my credit and provided me with a line of credit. All of that helped me to be able to grow my business by allowing me to purchase the things I needed to promote my business.

The one thing you have to be mindful of is that everyone wants to be paid. You want to get paid. Your business wants to get paid. The bank wants to get paid. The IRS will get paid!

My last piece of information in this chapter: I earned a small interest on my money for having it in the bank. I didn't even know the bank was using my money to grow the bank. Yet, I did not complain. I see the interest as free money. Well…until they stop paying it, then HOUSTON, we have a problem!

Chapter 17

Subcontracting

Most of us who are starting out as a full-time artist can't afford to hire employees. We can barely afford to hire ourselves. Subcontracting is a good option. In layman terms, subcontracting is when you hire someone (i.e. vendor, independent contractor or freelancer) who is not an employee of your company to do a particular service like building a website or answering the phone.

Companies of all sizes outsource. The reason for me writing about it here is because most of us who are just starting out as a full-time artist can't afford to hire employees. We can't even afford to hire ourselves.

However, we are in a delicate situation because we can't do everything we need to do. I tried and you only find out that you have made a mistake or you're constantly trying to keep up with yourself. In short, you may start a lot of things but nothing is completely finished. You may find yourself not being good with technology but you're trying to build your own website. Whew. That is hard. You own a camera so you taking selfies and saying that they are headshots! You should be focused on perfecting your craft and bringing in the money.

Subcontracting is a way to get a lot of the tasks you need completed done. Before the work starts you should have a contract in writing and signed by both parties. Your Art Is Your Empire so you'll both need to have a clear understanding and a contractual agreement outlining each person's responsibility. You don't want the subcontractor to just quit your project. Your contract will be legal and will hold up in court. You want to say, "If you quit, I'm going to sue you". You may be bluffing but the subcontractor doesn't know. If the contractor fails to fulfill the contract, you have the option to sue the person as long as they have agreed, in writing, to complete the work. This is more legally binding than both parties having a verbal agreement. I know you are probably saying you're going to only work with people you can trust. I believe you but sometimes they get offered more money to do the same work for someone else.

You can almost always find people who are skilled at doing the tasks you need done amongst your family, friends, online resources, and networking. The beauty is that someone is looking to build their portfolio or resume or client list and they usually have reasonable prices. You have to compare prices to get the best deal but you should also be more concerned with the quality of their previous works. Ask to see samples or references. If you can contact someone that used the contractor's services, you can find out if the person was pleased with the work. If references aren't available and you are the first person hiring them, they should still provide samples to show you what they are capable of doing.

Here is where subcontracting becomes important. You can put in writing exactly what you are hiring this person to do, what the final project should look like, how long it should take to complete, and what the quality should be. Feel free to include in your contract how many drafts you are allowed, how long it should take, and how the contract can be void. You should also write in this agreement everything you want for your money. I don't care how much of a discount you are getting or how this person is just starting out. You want what you need because if this person doesn't meet your criteria, you still need the job completed.

The contractor has the right to ask you to change or add certain things to this agreement, which is fine as long as you choose to agree to those terms. Typically, subcontractors ask for partial payment or a deposit, before they begin. They may also ask for a non-refundable down payment just in case you change your mind.

I know most of us just starting out can't afford a lawyer to draw up contracts but you can find sample contracts online. Your local government office may have samples for you to choose from. The Small Business Administration Office or SBA website is a great source and usually has samples available for download.

Another huge benefit in hiring subcontractors is using your money to grow your business. If you hire employees, you'll have to pay Social Security taxes, workers' compensation benefits, or health insurance, etc. You'll reach this stage eventually but in the beginning, you should focus on building your brand.

Chapter 18

The Confidentiality Agreement

A confidentiality agreement also known, as a non-disclosure agreement is basically an agreement that tells folks to keep their mouths closed about your inventions, products, or ideas before you are ready to make those things public. It is best to have people sign confidentiality agreements before you tell them your secrets.

If you were planning to work with a group of folks, you would have to make each person sign an individual agreement. One person should not sign for a whole group, company or organization. Each individual has to be held accountable separately. For instance, you are in the recording studio with your engineer, producer, and the studio staff. They're waiting in the studio for you to start your recording session for your latest CD. You should ask each of them to sign a confidentiality agreement not to discuss your CD title, the title of the new tracks, or what the tracks are about. The agreement should also include that no one is allowed to let anyone listen to the tracks, see the lyric sheet, or listen to the beats.

I know you have heard of situations when someone's entire album or track was leaked via the Internet. The problem with that is you may lose money. If you wanted to release the CD or track for sale online on a certain date but it was leaked for free, you lose potential royalties and album sales. It's possible the leaker could financially benefit from it if he/she sold it to a source that leaked it to the public. Protect yourself and your work. Have a confidentiality agreement available that specifies your confidentiality needs. The financial penalties for violation of the contract are listed in the contract that is issued to the individuals. A steep enough financial penalties can keep folks honest and their mouths closed.

I know you are only going to work with people you can trust. However, you can never tell who will just have a casual conversation with their friends, girlfriends or whomever. Of course, the person they tell starts telling other people. To keep things quiet make them sign the contracts.

Remember, you have to be very specific on what should be kept under wraps. It may be hard or too confusing to prove in court how they have violated the agreement if you make it too broad. Also allow the individuals enough time to have the details in your contracts read or reviewed by each individual or their attorneys' before they sign the agreement.

The agreement should also make clear who owns the material; information, idea and what should be confidential. You also want to include how long the agreement lasts, whether it is a few days, a few weeks, a few months, a few years, or indefinitely.

In contracts, you can include what information can be discussed. In one case, let's say you are working with a producer per your agreement, and another person begins to ask about upcoming projects, the producer can say that he is working with you on a new project but that's all he can tell the person. If you want, you can allow him to say what artists are featured on the project. Or you can restrict him from saying anything; it's totally up to you. However, allowing him to say who is on the project can help create great buzz and excitement, but you have to have the featured artists sign a confidentiality agreement that forbids them from discussing the specifics as well. You can allow them to say something like, "Yea. We're in the studio. The tracks are going to blow ya minds." You can also prevent the artist from saying that. You have control over this. You say what can and cannot be discussed.

It doesn't matter if you are not paying anyone, if they are working with you on your material, information, products or ideas, you can have them silenced with the contract. The confidentiality agreement needs to be signed before you tell them anything. If you allow them to work on your projects or disclose confidential material before signing an agreement, they can refuse to sign anything and not be liable for keeping your projects secret. So keep your mouth closed until all parties read through it and sign the agreement. Don't forget to state the penalties of breaching your contract and indicate which laws the contract is protected by. Do not be fearful that the other person(s) will lose interest in helping you because this is your art. It is part of your empire so you must protect it. If they have a problem signing it, that could suggest that they have a problem keeping their mouths closed. Good to find out about bad apples before you bite into them.

Chapter 19

The Website

I think websites are an amazing marketing tool. Websites are a great way to be available to your fans when you are not actually present. Having a website helps you get out the messages you want about you and your work. Communicate directly with your fans through your blogs, pictures, and videos, give exclusive updates, as well as provide information on services and products you offer. Post your performance schedule.

You'll be amazed at how many people who have seen your performances and follow up and do an online search to find out more about you. This usually results in "Word-of-mouth" promotion and you'll be surprised by how many more will do an online search of you. Having a website gives them the opportunity to discover you, which could lead to more paid opportunities.

A website is a must have. The only drawback that I have with a website is when you pay a web developer to create it and host it. You cannot control how soon they update your site. However, there are many companies that offer website templates where you can customize and update at reasonable prices or in some cases, free. All you have to do is choose the template you like and add pictures and text where you want it. You can access it as much as you want, re-arrange what you like or don't like, and most importantly update as often as you need.

If you are going to use a template from a website, I suggest you pay for it. If you use a free template and hosting, the hosting company name will come first. You will more than likely have unwanted advertisements on your site that you are not being paid to host. When purchasing a web address, use your stage name or business name. This makes it even easier to find you when people are searching for you.

You can tag your website with names associated with what you do and even use your company name, or your name. Doing this will help bring your website closer to the top of Internet search engines when someone decides to do further research on your craft. For example: you are Jim Smith and you are an acrylic painter from Atlanta. Your company's name is Acrylic God. I would tag each page with acrylic painting, acrylic painter, acrylic art, Atlanta artist, and Atlanta acrylic painter. Jim Smith, Jim's acrylic, God, Acrylic God, drawing, painting, etc.

You get my point. I made mention earlier of using your stage name when naming your website. If your birth name is Jim Smith and you use Acrylic God as your stage name, I would name my website Acrylic God. I would make my website address <u>acrylicgod.com</u>. No one is looking for Jim Smith if they know you as Acrylic God. Remember, your goal is to make money. You are a full-time artist so you have to eat…everyday or you'll die.

Another suggestion is when you go to purchase your web address, do not listen to that voice in your head that says, "Oh, wow. I can use www.acrylicgod.us.com, or www.acrylicgod.tk or whatever you see that seems brand new. I did that. It sucks. The majority of people who have websites use the extensions .com, org, and .net. When searching the Internet, most people are accustomed to using .com in their search. Therefore, keep it simple. Help them find you. The other thing is if you use something else outside of .com, someone else can purchase www.acrylic.god.com and use it for a baby wipe website or worse a porn site! Imagine what the people who find these sites will think about you! Chances are, they may not remember you said www.acrylic.god.skip. They will only remember the other sites they visited in the past with the commonly used .com and will apply .com to the site instead of .skip. Just something for you to think about.

One last note, and a great thing to do, you can link your social media sites to your website. If the settings are done right, whatever you post to your website will be made visible and post to all linked social media platforms. So for your friends who may have forgotten that you are an artist, they'll be reminded via the post which will lead them to your website. The more hits to your website, the better.

Chapter 20

Social Media

This chapter's focus is on a business social media page and not a personal page. Social media is an awesome FREE way to brand and market your services and products. It is also a great way to communicate directly with your fans. Social media is a unique way to target people, companies and events that you are interested in doing business with. There are CEOs of major companies to the lower level staffers on popular social media sites that you can connect with.

I suggest you post your bio in your profile. I would include my email, website, and photos but not my personal phone number. People will call and it may be for reasons that are not related to your business.

You have to be careful with photos. I would post photos that are respectful and relevant to the branding of my business. I would also show the relaxed pictures of me and/ or members of my staff celebrating an accomplishment, a retreat, and other pictures that show a softer and fun side of the company and its employees. However, the business pictures will dominate. Make sure you keep the private chats professional as well. I do not want people to lose sight that this is a company and we offer certain products and services. I am not saying to jam this down their throats, but you want it to be clear that you are a business. Sometimes people forget or misunderstand where the line between your friendship with them and your business is drawn. You cannot make a living if your social media friends or friends in general expect your products and services to be free for them. You have to remind them that there is a line. If they respect you, they will pay you. They should want to see you succeed.

When a new product or service is available, I will post it. When there is a sale, I will post it. If we have received great reviews, news coverage, or released a new video, I will post it. Everything that shows my accomplishments, the company or the staff is newsworthy.

I will only post a status or picture once or twice a day unless we have an event or a limited sale. We want to shoot a reminder to people. That will be done in moderation as well.

Be mindful of the kind of friend request you accept. It may be considered very unprofessional or less like a business page if your timeline is plastered with personal provocative situations and poses of your "friends".

Remember, social media is now a medium used by professionals seeking out potential people clients and service providers such as you.

Now when reaching out to people, I would suggest you send a friend request with a message that briefly introduces you.

Example: "Hi. My name is Lamont Carey. I am a spoken word artist from Washington, DC. I'm sending you this friend request because I admire your work with spoken word artists. It would be awesome to have an opportunity to network with you." Flattery gets you places. (LOL). Most people accept whoever sends them a request regardless but being polite and recognizing their accomplishments could get you a reply message. Once the request is accepted, I would send them a thank you message with further praise and a question all wrapped in one. I would say something like, "Mr/Mrs (name), I love how you were so instrumental in guiding the successful careers of BOOM BOOM. I too am a spoken word artist. I'm currently looking for representation and wondered what you look for in an artist? Thank you again for allowing me to network with you. I'm looking forward to your reply." We all like flattery and we like to know you did your research. Additionally, we all like to give advice on how to approach us! You were polite and professional. I would wait for a few weeks for a reply. If you hear nothing after a few weeks, then I would follow up with this," I know you're a very busy individual. This message is just a brief reminder regarding an inquiry I sent you on such and such day. I'd like to ask one more question. Is there a preferred method to contact you in regards to representation? I want to go through the proper channels if you just let me know the web address or contact number." After this, I would be done with contacting this person unless they reply and tell me what to do.

I have received plenty of messages like such,

"Yo Lamont! I'm the hottest spoken word artist in New York! Lets connect and get this paper!"

'Lamont check out my spoken word videos and tell me what you think."

I respect their desire to make their dreams a reality but you have to DO BUSINESS when you are trying to DO BUSINESS. First impressions can really be a good or bad thing and are lasting.

Regardless if you never get a reply message from anyone, you still have to promote you. I made tons of mistakes in the beginning. I still make them but not as often and definitely not the same ones. The one thing I hate on

social media sites is people tagging me in EVERYTHING.
I'll look at the tag but more than likely, I will un-tag myself
if it is not relevant to my empire or me.

When you post on your pages, I think one or two
posts a day is good to begin capturing the attention of folks.
I stop paying attention if you are posting all day. You lose
people instead of gaining their interest with too many posts.
If you post something I like, I will comment or like it, and
hence, I am paying attention to what I relate to. If you post
a video with a catchy title, I will take a listen. If I like it, I
will hit the like button or share with my network.

My point is even though we are on the worldwide
web, and privacy seems to be a thing of the past, people
still want some distance. I give them their space because I
will engage when they post something I like or reach out to
me in a way that is respectful.

Remember, you are on social media to further build
your Empire. Do not get sidetracked into arguing and doing
other things that will eventually hurt your business image.

Chapter 21

The Press kit

The press kit is a wonderful way to tell your story in the most exciting way. In other words, it is an effective way to sell yourself and/or your company. A press kit is generally a synopsis or summary of your company. However, you want to make it interesting and fun. Do not make the synopsis or summary wordy and do use pictures to make it more appealing. Professional quality photos are a must.

You should make the press kit available electronically and in hardcopy. Let's take look at both formats:

Electronic Press Kit:

1. Your press kit should have an **Overview** of what your company does. The length of this overview should be at least a half page or one page maximum. In the overview, I would include:

When you got started?

Why you started?

And some of your biggest achievements.

LaCarey Enterprises, LLC was created in 2014 to assist and motivate at-risk youth, ex-offenders, and artists in developing skills to fulfill their true passions and live out their dreams in the entertainment industry or starting businesses. The company originally started in 2005 as LaCarey Entertainment, LLC. Our creative services further attracted the attention of governments, at-risks youth programs, and correctional facilities due to our founder's unique way to using the arts to solve real-life problems and help folks to make better decisions.

Since the creation of the company we have casted individuals in critically acclaimed shows such as HBO's THE WIRE, Def Poetry Jam, and Centric's Lyric Cafe. We have inspired thousands of youth, incarcerated individuals and former prisoners to realize their true passions. Many have gone on to start their own companies, as well as, become authors, actors, and performers.

2. Your **Biography** also known as **Bio** should be no more than a page long. It is similar to the overview but more of the focus is on you, the artist. You can mention where you're from, how long you have been an artist, your artistic accomplishments, etc. Many artists mention that their work can be compared to so it gives the reader something to connect to.

Lamont Carey was born in Washington, DC, but raised in prison. He discovered the arts while incarcerated and it has changed his life. He is currently an internationally known spoken word artist, motivational speaker, playwright, and author.

Many people compare his rawness to the likes of Tupac and DMX because his work reflects the heartbeat of urban survival. The passion in his unique delivery makes the images vivid and living.

His style of spoken word has landed him features on HBO's Def Poetry Jam, THE WIRE and Centric's Lyric Cafe. As a playwright, his work has been featured at the John F. Kennedy Center. His motivational speaking abilities have allowed him to speak to thousands of students, prisoners, ex-offenders and, communities around the United States. As a result of his writing, Lamont released four critically acclaimed books, two from his prison series, The Wall and The Hill and his poetry book, Reach Into My Darkness. His poetry book is currently being used in public schools to encourage critical thinking in students. His latest project, Your Art Is Your Empire, is a self-help book for artists on how to turn their craft into a profitable business.

Lamont Carey has been awarded Poet of the Year, Best Community Poet, Visionary Award, Good Black Man Award, Congressional Award, and Senate Award winner.

Lamont Carey leaves a lasting impact on individuals and people via his thoughts, vocally or in print.

Short and sweet.

You should also include **links to news stories also known as press** that were written about you or mentions your work and its impact. You'd have to go through a process to try and get permission to reprint articles but if you are later granted the reprints, use only one or two articles. If you have five links, use them. I would give a brief summary, no more than three sentences, of each for the links that are shown. Example:

The Washington Post did an article on the celebratory mood of the audience, who gave me a standing ovation at the Vatican, after my twenty-minute performance composed of my latest material.

This summary left me curious. I want to know what the world renown Washington Post wrote about you. It is even more amazing that you performed at the Vatican and you just happened to have a picture of the Pope giving you a standing ovation. Or not.

Of course your articles do not have to be this glorious. You just need to include them if you have any. People need to see that the media is interested in you enough to write articles. If you do not have any articles, do not worry. I know folks will be writing about you soon enough. For now, just skip that section and move on.

4. You want to leave **Contact Information**. This information should include if available:

Email

Phone

Website

Mailing address.

Social media contact

Your email is important because most people prefer to communicate this way. It may be more efficient for them to email you than to call. Make sure you have one.

124

In my opinion your email should include your company's name or your name. It should be easy to spell and remember. If it's not, your opportunity can end up in the wrong email box. If it is not associated with your name or your company name, it may be difficult to remember especially if someone does not have your press kit or business card handy. Additionally, using your name or your business name is further branding your company. Bam!

Your phone number is equally important. There are some folks who prefer to call you, your agent, or manager so they will not have to continue emailing back and forth. Some people want to make sure they like your personality or that you are professional. With that being said, please do not have an unclear and profanity-filled voice-mail message. It is a turn-off and it is not professional. Have a pleasant voice that is polite and straight to the point.

You have reached Lamont Carey, President of LaCarey Enterprises, LLC. I am sorry I wasn't able to take your call but if you leave me a brief message stating your reason for calling and a contact number, I will return your call as soon as possible. (BEEP)"

Another thing, this phone is the heartbeat of your business. If this is not a priority, you may end up standing at the corner with that cup in your hand trying to bum some change. This phone should never be disconnected or the number changed. Choose this phone over groceries because when this phone rings, chances are it will lead to money to buy groceries. Do not allow your toddler, crazy friends, and family members to answer this phone. Protect this phone. Some opportunities may call five years later. This is also not the phone number to give out when you are dating. You cannot change this number when the stalker keeps calling.

I highly recommend you save the press kit in a format that cannot be edited by someone other than your staff. Remember, you can include a different photo of you or your staff on every section to make it more appealing. Also, keep it short and sweet.

The physical copy of your press kit is exactly the same. The only exception is that you should keep these sheets of paper inside of a nice folder that is branded with your company colors and logo. You do not have to buy very expensive folders but you should not use folders that will fall apart or will wear fast.

I hope you enjoyed this book. Please visit my website, (lacareyenterprises.com), and leave a short review or you can do it on amazon.com.

Thanks for all of your support! Send me a letter letting me know if this helped you. Volume two will be on the way and titled, How To Make Money Off Spoken word. While geared toward those in the spoken word industry, the next book can be applied to any artist in any medium.

THE END

Listed below are other projects and services currently available from Lamont Carey. All products are available electronically on most major book retailers' website as well as Nooks and Kindles. Order from www.lacareyenterprises.com to receive an autographed copy.

Lamont Carey is also a motivational speaker, workshop facilitator, consultant and more. Visit our website to book him for your international or national event. He provides services to government agencies, for-profit and nonprofit organizations, schools, Colleges, re-entry programs, book clubs, penal systems for youth and adults and more. Contact us to arrange to have Lamont Carey get involved with your program or events.

IMAGINE

Lamont Carey's award winning CD containing such hits as "I Can't Read", "Confidence", "I Hate This Place", "She Says She Loves Me", and ten other electrifying spoken word pieces.

THE HILL. Follow Sherman as he begins serving his prison sentence at Lorton Correctional Compound. This complex houses some of the deadliest men in the world. It's a penitentiary so dangerous that other maximum-security prisoners don't wanna go. Sherman made some bad choices in his life. Now he will either live or die from the consequences.

THE WALL is the sequel to the book THE HILL. It takes you to a prison more deadly and sinister than THE HILL. Real Gangsters have been known to scream behind…THE WALL. No one is safe. There are no leaders. Everyone is a killer.

Reach Into My Darkness is a collection of poems that focus on youth issues. Teachers are using this book to get students to express themselves, to think outside of the box and become better decision-makers. It touches on diverse issues that include bullying, peer pressure and education.

Learning To Be A Mommy-The Play (DVD)

Lamont Carey's second play directed at the John F. Kennedy Center is a story about a young girl who struggles while making sure her family is safe, healthy, and protected. She has to make some choices that could leave her dead and her family destroyed.

Upcoming projects from Lamont Carey

How to Make Money From Spoken Word

The Business Side of Spokenword. This book is a blueprint on how to maximize your money making potential as an artist. It covers everything from protecting your work to marketing it.

Capers

Drug dealers are never safe because someone always want what they have. Skinny, Ajax and Nut wants exactly what a drug dealer has. They decided to go and get it. You can never walk quietly away from a robbery. Either a gun is fired during or soon after it happens. A war is guaranteed to break out but between who, the robbers and the victim or between the robbers? Somebody is going to pull the trigger.

The Redeemer

It's a story about the anti-Christ coming into the world as Jesus Christ. His goal is to convince the world to kneel in union to him in prayer. This would open the gates of Hell and allow Satan to rule over the world. The one way to expose and stop him may not be revealed in time!

Laws Of The STREET

(The novel series & TV series)

A story about a community that is forced to live under the rules set by the criminals. This is a look into the lives of those who want to escape, those who don't believe their are other options, and those who like it just the way things are.

Outside The Gate

This is a documentary about the struggles, strategies, and triumphs of four ex-offenders who faced an enormous amount of obstacles but are determined to succeed. Four different lives. Four different failures. Four different stories. and just maybe four different successes.

To make arrangements internationally, nationally or locally to have Lamont Carey involved in your upcoming projects or events for your groups, students, prisoners, employees, conferences, etc, contact us at:

lacareymanagement@sagmail.com

You may visit the website at:

www.lacareyenterprises.com

Send fan mail to:

LaCarey Entertainment, LLC

P.O. Box 64256

Washington, DC 20029